Essential Mathematics for Life

BOOK 1

Whole Numbers

Fourth
Edition

GLENCOE
McGraw-Hill

New York, New York
Columbus, Ohio
Mission Hills, California
Peoria, Illinois

Authors

Mary S. Charuhas
Associate Dean
College of Lake County
Grayslake, Illinois

Dorothy McMurtry
District Director of ABE,GED,
    ESL
City Colleges of Chicago
Chicago, Illinois

The Mathematics Faculty
American Preparatory Institute
Killeen, Texas

Contributing Writers

Kathryn S. Harr
Mathematics Instructor
Pickerington, Ohio

Priscilla Ware
Educational Consultant and
    Instructor
Columbus, Ohio

Dr. Pearl Chase
Professional Consultants of Dallas
Cedar Hill, Texas

Contributing Editors and Reviewers

Barbara Warner
Monroe Community College
Rochester, New York

Michelle Heatherly
Coastal Carolina Community
    College
Jacksonville, North Carolina

Anita Armfield
York Technical College
Rock Hill, South Carolina

Judy D. Cole
Lafayette Regional Technical
    Institute
Lafayette, Louisiana

Mary Fincher
New Orleans Job Corps
New Orleans, Louisiana

Cheryl Gunderson
Rusk Community Learning
    Center
Ladysmith, Wisconsin

Cynthia A. Love
Columbus City Schools
Columbus, Ohio

Joyce Claar
South Westchester BOCES
Valhalla, New York

John Grabowski
St. Joseph Hill Academy
Staten Island, New York

Virginia Victor
Maple Run Youth Center
Cumberland, Maryland

Sandi Braga
College of South Idaho
Twin Falls, Idaho

Maggie Cunningham
Adult Education
Schertz, Texas

Sylvia Gilliard
Naval Consolidated Brig
Charleston, South Carolina

Eva Eaton-Smith
Cecil Community College
Elkton, Maryland

Fabienne West
John C. Calhoun State
    Community College
Decatur, Alabama

Photo credits: Cover, ©Ralph Mercer/Tony Stone Images; 6, Brent Turner/BLT Productions;
18, file photo; 27, Brent Turner/BLT Productions; 28, ©Jeffrey Sylvester/FPG International;
63, ©Gerard Fritz/FPG International; 101, Brent Turner/BLT Productions; courtesy Callender
Cleaners, Bexley, OH; 104, Mak-One Photo Design; 113, Brent Turner/BLT Productions;
115, Brent Turner/BLT Productions, courtesy Connell's Flowers, Bexley, OH; 125, Brent
Turner/BLT Productions; 137, Brent Turner/BLT Productions, courtesy Kids 4 U, Reynolds-
burg, OH; 144, Brent Turner/BLT Productions; 147, Brent Turner/BLT Productions, courtesy
Eastland Career Center, Groveport, OH; 158, Brent Turner/BLT Productions, courtesy Eastland Career Center, Groveport, OH; 181, ©Bob Daemmrich/Stock Boston.

Send all inquiries to:
Glencoe/McGraw-Hill
936 Eastwind Drive
Westerville, Ohio 43081

ISBN: 0-02-802608-X

1 2 3 4 5 6 7 8 9 POH 02 01 00 99 98 97 96 95 94

C O N T E N T S

Addition and Subtraction

Unit 1 Place Value

Unit 2 Addition and Subtraction Basic Facts

Unit 3 Addition

Unit 4 Subtraction

Unit 5 Multiplication and Division Basic Facts

Unit 6 Multiplying

Unit 7 Dividing

Unit 8 Using Whole Number Skills

Place Value

Write the numbers or words.

1. twenty-three _____   2. sixty-eight _____   3. ninety-two _____

4. 47 _____   5. 81 _____   6. 56 _____

How many thousands, hundreds, tens, and ones?

7. 4,679   _____ thousands   _____ hundreds   _____ tens   _____ ones

8. 9,067   _____ thousands   _____ hundreds   _____ tens   _____ ones

9. 4,890   _____ thousands   _____ hundreds   _____ tens   _____ ones

Write the numbers or words.

10. Fifty thousand, four hundred ninety-eight _____

11. Eight hundred million, seven thousand, four hundred seven _____

12. 1,492 _____

13. 9,070 _____

Fill in the blanks with > or <.

14. 56 _____ 47   **15.** 111 _____ 101   **16.** 3,402 _____ 3,302

Put these numbers in order from smallest to largest.

17. 567   657   765   576   **18.** 5,089   5,090   5,900   5,908

_____ _____ _____ _____   _____ _____ _____ _____

Write the digits in the ten thousands place.

19. 34,672   _____   **20.** 937,501   _____   **21.** 1,521,091   _____

What numbers are in the hundred thousands place?

22. 1,543,907   _____   **23.** 32,894,401   _____   **24.** 453,098,194   _____

What numbers are in the ten millions place?

25. 356,890,123   _____   **26.** 841,509,732   _____   **27.** 789,123,456   _____

Round the number to the nearest thousand and nearest hundred.

28. 555,784   thousand _____   hundred _____

Round the number to the nearest million and ten thousand.

29. 35,908,877 million _____   ten thousand _____

Problem Solving

Solve the following problems.

30. A big-screen TV costs $1,679 at A's Electronics. The same TV costs $1,685 at B's Electronics. Which store has the better price?   _____

31. Mac's business files are coded by number. Put his files in order from the smallest to the largest number: 362, 197, 464, 58, 102, 591, 179, 463, 85, and 221.   _____

32. Nan took 5 math tests. Put her scores in order from the highest to the lowest: 93, 67, 87, 79, and 91.   _____

2

Place Value—Ones and Tens

Numbers are made up of digits. The position of the digit in the number shows the digit's place value. This place value can be in the ones place or the tens place.

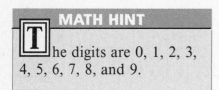

MATH HINT

The digits are 0, 1, 2, 3, 4, 5, 6, 7, 8, and 9.

Examples

A. twenty-four

2 tens   4 ones
20   +   4

24
tens place ↑↑ ones place

B. forty

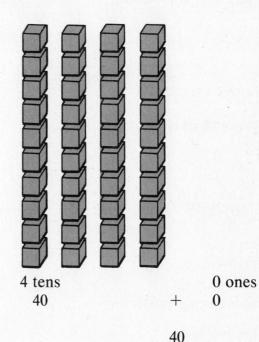

4 tens   0 ones
40   +   0

40
tens place ↑↑ ones place

Write the numbers.

1. 1 ten   _10_   2. 6 tens   _____

3. 2 tens   _____   4. 7 tens   _____

5. 3 tens   _____   6. 8 tens   _____

7. 4 tens   _____   8. 9 tens   _____

9. 5 tens   _____   10. 10 tens   _100_

11. $20 + 3 =$ _____   12. $60 + 7 =$ _____

13. $50 + 6 =$ _____   14. $90 + 1 =$ _____

How many tens and ones?

15. 87 = _____ tens _____ ones   16. 60 = _____ tens _____ ones

17. 49 = _____ tens _____ ones   18. 78 = _____ tens _____ ones

Write these numbers.

19. forty-eight   _____   20. thirty-nine   _____

21. ninety-three   _____   22. twenty-six   _____

23. sixty-two   _____   24. fifty   _____

25. seventy-seven   _____   26. eighty-three   _____

Write the words.

27. 29 _twenty-nine_   28. 42 _____

29. 99 _____   30. 76 _____

31. 65 _____   32. 53 _____

33. 30 _____   34. 86 _____

Circle the numbers with

35. 6 in the tens place

26 (62) 56 (68) 36

36. 2 in the ones place

28 82 42 92 12

37. 9 in the ones place

89 98 79 95 94

38. 4 in the tens place

34 45 54 49 94

39. 8 in the tens place

78 89 18 82 88

40. 3 in the ones place

39 63 84 23 93

41. 6 in the ones place

67 76 56 63 16

42. 9 in the tens place

89 90 94 69 93

43. 1 in the tens place

17 71 81 14 12

44. 5 in the ones place

53 62 75 14 25

Write these numbers as a sum of tens and ones.

45. 22 = _20_ + _2_

46. 26 = _____ + _____

47. 62 = _____ + _____

48. 66 = _____ + _____

49. 71 = _____ + _____

50. 98 = _____ + _____

51. 82 = _____ + _____

52. 16 = _____ + _____

53. 33 = _____ + _____

54. 77 = _____ + _____

55. 43 = _____ + _____

56. 51 = _____ + _____

57. 34 = _____ + _____

58. 94 = _____ + _____

59. 13 = _____ + _____

Using Numbers in a Street Address

Most city addresses have numbers and a street name. The numbers help you find a building.

Buildings with numbers in the same hundreds are usually on the same block. This means that stores with the addresses **801** and **825** Grove Street are usually on the same block. They have the same number **8** in the hundreds place.

However, 725 Grove Street and 431 Grove Street are not in the same block. They are three blocks apart (7 − 4 = 3).

Odd numbers (numbers ending in **1, 3, 5, 7,** or **9**) are on one side of the street.

Even numbers (numbers ending in **0, 2, 4, 6,** or **8**) are on the other side.

Circle pairs of addresses that are on the same block.

1. 1512 N. Oak 1894 N. Oak	**2.** 817 W. Peach 819 W. Peach	**3.** 6578 S. Main 4325 S. Main	**4.** 140 W. Ohio 12 W. Ohio
5. 1907 E. Elm 20 E. Elm	**6.** 16 N. Church 18 N. Church	**7.** 509 E. Maple 514 E. Maple	**8.** 2345 E. Pine 2276 E. Pine

Circle pairs of addresses that are on the same side of the street.

9. 2020 Ave. A 2224 Ave. A	**10.** 301 E. North 310 E. North	**11.** 516 S. Penn 918 S. Penn	**12.** 3908 Valjean 3749 Valjean

13. 730 Worth St.   **14.** 8765 Mozart   **15.** 23 Court Ave.   **16.** 1415 Knight
648 Worth St.   6542 Mozart   145 Court Ave.   207 Knight

How many blocks must you walk

17. if you start at 1600 Main Street and walk to 1800 Main Street?

_____ blocks

18. if you start at 340 First Street and walk to 1010 First Street?

_____ blocks

19. if you start at 2300 South Place and walk to 2800 South Place?

_____ blocks

20. if you start at 500 Avenue N and walk to 1200 Avenue N?

_____ blocks

Solve the following problems.

21. Josie's house is located at 846 Easton Road. Her friend, Sasha, lives at 1024 Easton Road. Are they on the same block?

_____

22. If Thomas moved from 158 Vine Street to 165 Vine Street, did he move to the same side of Vine Street or across the street?

_____

23. If Jerome's address is 1224 South 4th Street and his sister lives next door, what is her address?

(a) 225 South 4th Street

(b) 1226 South 4th Street

_____

24. If Amanda's school is located at 560 James Avenue, and her house is at 1220 James Avenue, how many blocks does she walk to school?

_____

7

Place Value—Hundreds and Thousands

Beyond the ones and tens place, place value can be in the hundreds or thousands place. Remember to put a comma after any number in the thousands place: **3,000   4,896**

Examples

A. Three hundred sixty-four

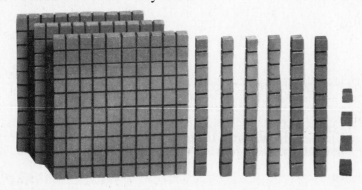

3 hundreds   + 6 tens   +4 ones
300   + 60   +4

                3   6   4

hundreds place ———↑   ↑   ↑——— ones place
               tens place

B. One thousand, three hundred sixty-four

1 thousand   + 3 hundreds   + 6 tens   + 4 ones
1,000   + 300   + 60   + 4

               1,   3   6   4

thousands place ——↑   ↑   ↑   ↑—— ones place
       hundreds place ——↑   └— tens place

How many hundreds, tens, and ones?

1. 307 ___ hundreds ___ tens ___ ones   2. 739 ___ hundreds ___ tens ___ ones

3. 450 ___ hundreds ___ tens ___ ones   4. 698 ___ hundreds ___ tens ___ ones

How many thousands, hundreds, tens, and ones?

5. 3,456   __3__ thousands __4__ hundreds __5__ tens __6__ ones

6. 5,073   ___ thousands ___ hundreds ___ tens ___ ones

7. 4,389   ___ thousands ___ hundreds ___ tens ___ ones

8. 7,902   ___ thousands ___ hundreds ___ tens ___ ones

Circle the numbers with

9. 8 in the hundreds place   10. 4 in the thousands place
   908   (809)   (899)   987   404   4,873   5,483   4,442

11. 2 in the hundreds place   12. 1 in the thousands place
    4,290   5,402   2,285   267   4,197   1,100   1,010   910

Write the words or numbers.

13. 1,349 _one thousand, three-hundred forty-nine_

14. 3,504 _____

15. 6,042 _____

16. 7,390 _____

17. two thousand, four hundred eighty-five   _____

18. seven thousand, three   __2,485__

19. three thousand, two hundred seven   _____

20. six thousand, one hundred   _____

Comparing and Ordering Numbers

The **digits** are 0, 1, 2, 3, 4, 5, 6, 7, 8, and 9. They are used in writing numbers. These signs are used when comparing numbers: < and >.

The symbol > means greater than.   The symbol < means less than.

Examples

A. 7 > 5 means
7 is **greater than 5.**

B. 5 < 7 means
5 is **less than 7.**

To compare large numbers, start by comparing the digits that have the largest place value. If they are the same, compare digits in the next place and so on until one digit is greater.

C. Which is greater, 356 or 365?
First, look at the hundreds place.
   3 5 6
   3 6 5
The 3's are the same.
Next, look at the tens place.
   3 **5** 6
   3 **6** 5
5 < 6
So, 356 < 365.
356 is less than 365.

> **MATH HINT**
> To order numbers, compare them to find the lowest. Then find each number that is one greater than the number before.

Practice

Put < or > in the blanks.

1. 4 __>__ 3   **2.** 3 __<__ 4   **3.** 40 _____ 30   **4.** 30 _____ 40

5. 70 _____ 90   **6.** 10 _____ 14   **7.** 16 _____ 34   **8.** 64 _____ 46

9. 135 _____ 136   **10.** 759 _____ 859   **11.** 385 _____ 853   **12.** 499 _____ 587

13. 4,398 _____ 4,399   **14.** 2,906 _____ 2,806   **15.** 9,999 _____ 9,909

Write the numbers that are one greater.

16. 2, _3_ **17.** 34, _____ **18.** 89, _____ **19.** 364, _____

Write the numbers that are one less.

20. 8, _7_ **21.** 99, _____ **22.** 101, _____ **23.** 5,745, _____

Circle the highest price.

24.

| $5 | $8 | $11 |

25.

| $14 | $23 | $19 |

Circle the price that is more than $8.

26.

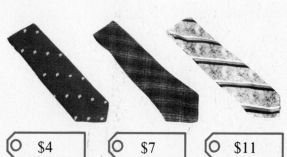

| $4 | $7 | $11 |

Circle the price that is less than $50.

27.

| $61 | $59 | $40 |

The arrows show room numbers down a hall. Should you go left or right to get to each room?

◁ 400–449   450–499 ▷

28. 402 _left_ **29.** 455 _____ **30.** 482 _____ **31.** 418 _____

32. 466 _____ **33.** 448 _____ **34.** 490 _____ **35.** 456 _____

Put these checks in order. Write the lowest number first.

Put these invoices in order. Write the lowest number first.

36. _____

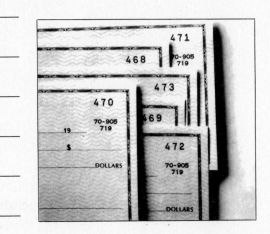

_____

_____

_____

_____

_____

37. _____

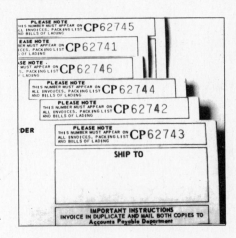

_____

_____

_____

_____

_____

_____

─────────────────── **Problem Solving** ───────────────────

Solve the following problems.

38. Scott saved $154. He wants to buy a new suit. Suit A costs $145; Suit B costs $155; Suit C costs $153. Which suit costs more than Scott saved?

_____

39. Ellen took four math tests. She scored 93, 73, 87, and 91. She is allowed to drop the lowest grade. Which grade can she drop?

_____

40. When Chris was building his deck, he put the boards in order from smallest to largest. The boards measured 55 inches, 60 inches, 58 inches, and 50 inches. Write the order from smallest to largest.

_____

41. The annual community play calls for a short adult to play the part of a child. Joe is 50 inches tall, Jay is 48 inches, Nate is 54 inches, and Matt is 47 inches tall. Who will get the part based on height?

_____

12

Writing Dates as Numbers

Starting with January, the months of the year are numbered from 1 to 12.

January	1	April	4	July	7	October	10
February	2	May	5	August	8	November	11
March	3	June	6	September	9	December	12

Many forms ask for the date in numbers. To write the date in numbers, first write the number of the month. Then write the day of the month. Then write the last two numbers of the year.

Some forms have two spaces each for month, day, and year. If you don't need two spaces for a month or a day, fill the extra space with a zero.

A. Write March 5, 1981, in numbers.

3/5/81   or   [0][3] [0][5] [8][1]

B. Write November 29, 1959, in numbers.

11/29/59   or   [1][1] [2][9] [5][9]

Write these dates in numbers or words.

1. November 28, 1965   ___/___/___   [ ][ ] [ ][ ] [ ][ ]

2. April 1, 1997   ___/___/___   [ ][ ] [ ][ ] [ ][ ]

3. December 31, 1984   ___/___/___   [ ][ ] [ ][ ] [ ][ ]

4. March 4, 1994   ___/___/___   [ ][ ] [ ][ ] [ ][ ]

5. 12/28/47   _____

6. 4/19/95   _____

7. [0][8] [0][5] [8][2]   _____

8. [1][2] [0][9] [8][8]   _____

Place Value to Hundred Millions

Below is a place value chart showing places up to hundred millions.

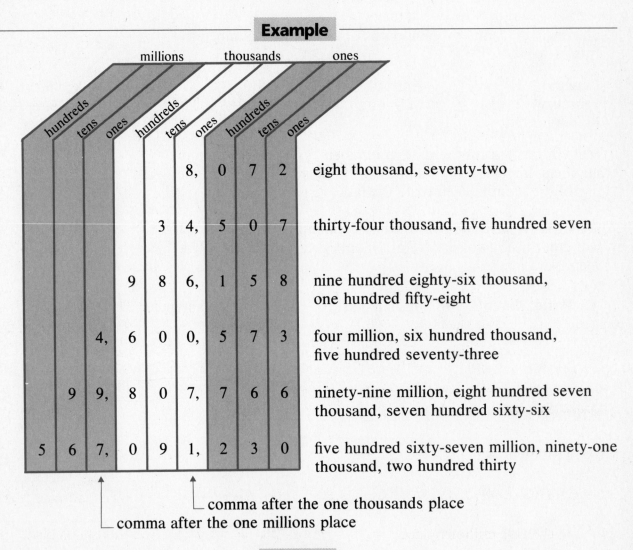

---- **Example** ----

					8,	0	7	2	eight thousand, seventy-two
			3	4,	5	0	7		thirty-four thousand, five hundred seven
		9	8	6,	1	5	8		nine hundred eighty-six thousand, one hundred fifty-eight
	4,	6	0	0,	5	7	3		four million, six hundred thousand, five hundred seventy-three
9	9,	8	0	7,	7	6	6		ninety-nine million, eight hundred seven thousand, seven hundred sixty-six
5	6	7,	0	9	1,	2	3	0	five hundred sixty-seven million, ninety-one thousand, two hundred thirty

↑ comma after the one millions place
↑ comma after the one thousands place

---- **Practice** ----

How many millions, thousands, ones?

1. 74,957,089   ___74___ millions ___957___ thousands ___89___ ones

2. 978,675,009   _____ millions _____ thousands _____ ones

3. 392,007,856   _____ millions _____ thousands _____ ones

What numbers are in the thousands place?

4. 64,083   _4_

5. 923,655   _____

6. 709,321   _____

What numbers are in the ten thousands place?

7. 35,678   _____

8. 345,890   _____

9. 23,495,867   _____

What numbers are in the hundred thousands place?

10. 2,309,675   _____

11. 345,678,901   _____

12. 845,902,761   _____

What numbers are in the one millions place?

13. 35,678,999   _____

14. 908,735,125   _____

15. 80,976,512   _____

What numbers are in the ten millions place?

16. 203,846,591   _____

17. 943,256,781   _____

18. 32,456,975   _____

What numbers are in the hundred millions place?

19. 908,716,534   _____

20. 100,400,500   _____

21. 762,904,813   _____

Circle the numbers with

22. 8 in the ten millions place

     387,890,642   890,768,003   980,732,500

23. 3 in the one thousands place

     304,892,403   939,763,984   34,852

24. 5 in the one millions place

     54,678,203   35,482,409   5,678,923

25. 7 in the hundred thousands place

     7,605,723   4,798,042   7,794,053

Write the numbers.

26. One million   _____

27. Ten thousand   _____

28. One hundred million

29. One hundred eleven million, eleven

      _____   _____

LIFE SKILL

Reading an Electric Meter

An electric meter shows how much electricity a customer uses. A set of five dials on the meter measures **kilowatt-hours.** It takes one kilowatt-hour of electricity to burn a 100-watt light bulb for 10 hours.

The electric company sends a **meter reader** around every so often to read the dials. The reading shows how much electricity was used since the last time a reading was taken.

You can check your own electric meter. Read the dials from left to right. When the pointer is between two numbers, read the smaller number. When the pointer is between 9 and 0, think of the 0 as 10.

Here is a set of readings from the Lankas' house. Write down the reading for each month. Then find the kilowatt-hours the Lankas used in April, May, June, and July. (Subtract the old reading from the current month.)

1. March 30   **Kilowatt-hours used**

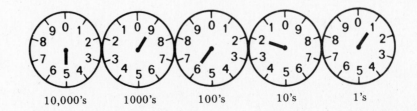

| 10,000's | 1000's | 100's | 10's | 1's |

 5 9 6 2 1

16

2. April 30

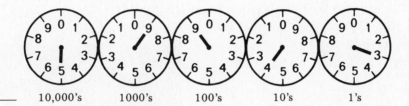

_____   10,000's   1000's   100's   10's   1's   _____

3. May 30

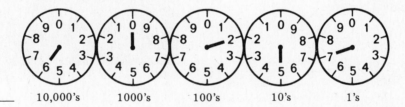

_____   10,000's   1000's   100's   10's   1's   _____

4. June 30

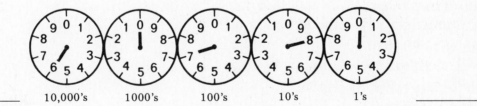

_____   10,000's   1000's   100's   10's   1's   _____

5. July 30

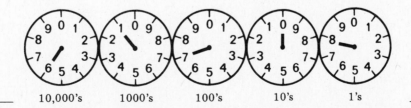

_____   10,000's   1000's   100's   10's   1's   _____

Rounding Numbers

Sometimes you don't need to know an exact number. You need to know "about" how many. A **rounded number** tells "about" how many.

There were 23,207 people at the game. A reporter for the local newspaper said, "About 23,000 people attended the game."

MATH HINT

U se the "Rule of 5" when you round.
If the place you are to round is 4 or less, then **round down.**
If the place you are to round is 5 or greater, then **round up.**

Look at this number line.

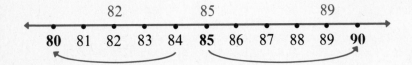

Rounding to the nearest ten

82 is closer to 80 than 90.
Since 2 is less than 5, you round 82 down to 80.

89 is closer to 90 than 80.
Since 9 is more than 5, you round 89 up to 90.

85 is halfway between 80 and 90.
You round 85 up to 90.

A. **Round 38 to the nearest ten.**
   Ask: Is 38 closer to 30 or 40?
   Look at the place to the right of the tens place. There is an 8.
   8 > 5. Round 38 to **40.**

B. **Round 314 to the nearest hundred.**
   Ask: Is 314 closer to 300 or 400?
   Look at the place to the right of the hundreds place. There is a
   1. 1 < 5. Round 314 to **300.**

C. **Round 19,452 to the nearest ten thousand.**
   Ask: Is 19,452 closer to 10,000 or 20,000?
   Look at the place to the right of the ten thousands place. There
   is a 9. 9 > 5. Round 19,452 to **20,000.**

D. **Round 23,652,415 to the nearest**

million	hundred thousand	thousand	hundred
24,000,000	23,700,000	23,652,000	23,652,400

—————————————————— **Practice** ——————————————————

Round to the nearest ten dollars.

1. $55 _____   2. $682 _____   3. $1,397 _____   4. $14,912 _____

Round to the nearest hundred dollars.

5. $427 _____   6. $862 _____   7. $5,567 _____

Round to the nearest

	thousand	hundred
8. 44,852	_____	_____
9. 98,590	_____	_____
10. 105,090	_____	_____

Round to the nearest

	million	ten thousand
11. 44,658,709	_____	_____
12. 304,565,988	_____	_____
13. 60,099,567	_____	_____

―――――――――――――― **Problem Solving** ――――――――――――――

Solve the following problems.

14. You have $752 in the bank. Round this amount to the nearest hundred dollars. _____

15. The car you want costs $6,870. Round this amount to the nearest thousand dollars. _____

16. The highest point on earth is Mt. Everest at 29,028 feet. Round to the nearest ten thousand feet. _____

17. The Russian Federation covers 625,000 square miles. Round to the nearest hundred thousand square miles. _____

18. It is 2,574 air miles from San Francisco to New York. Round to the nearest hundred air miles. _____

Problem Solving—Steps to Follow

Throughout this book and the other books in the series, you will be faced with problem solving lessons. Use the following steps to solve word problems.

Step 1 Read the problem and underline the key words. These words will usually relate to some mathematics reasoning computation.

Step 2 Make a plan to solve the problem. Ask yourself, Should I add, subtract, multiply, divide, round, or compare? You may have to do more than one of these operations for the same problem.

Step 3 Find the solution. Use your math knowledge to find your answer.

Step 4 Check the answer. Ask yourself, Is the answer reasonable? Did you find what you were asked for?

Example

Jose is saving to buy a car. He has saved $1,250. He found a car that costs $1,199. Has Jose saved enough money?

Follow these steps to solve the problem.

Step 1 Determine if Jose has saved enough money. The key words are **saved $1,250** and **car costs $1,199.**

Step 2 This problem asks you to compare the cost of the car and the amount saved.

Step 3 Find the solution. Which number is bigger? Can Jose afford to buy the car right now?

Since $1,250 > $1,199, he has more than enough money to buy the car.

Step 4 Check the answer. Is it reasonable that $1,250 is bigger than $1,199? Yes, by the ordering rules you learned in this unit.

Problem Solving

Solve the following problems.

1. When Tina went to the bank to cash her paycheck, she was given 4 ten-dollar bills. How much money was she given? _____

2. John filled out his time card for the week. He worked fifty-six hours this week. How did he write the time on his time card? _____

3. A stereo system costs $597 at Sam's. The same system costs $549 at Electronics Plus. Which store has the better deal? _____

4. Jamie needs to buy a new clothes dryer. The dryer costs $369. How many hundreds are in this cost? _____

   How many ones are in this cost? _____

5. At the Harris family reunion, the photographer asked the family to line up by age. Shane is 14, Jessie is 19, Tommy is 10, Bill is 35, and Margie is 31. Write the order of the people in the picture from youngest to oldest.

   _____

6. Theo paid three of his highest bills this week. His bills are: phone, $25; cable, $18; electric, $45; gas, $20; and rent $250. Which bills will Theo pay this week? _____

7. Kenny and Patrick were arguing which numbers were bigger. Kenny said one million. Patrick said one billion. Who was correct? _____

8. The budget for ABC Industries is $2,493,000 this year. What number is in the ten thousands place? _____

9. Mikey hopes to buy the house he is presently renting. The house sells for $75,499. Round this price to the nearest thousand. _____

10. You have $76 saved in the bank. Round this to the nearest ten. _____

Posttest

Write the numbers.

1. twelve _____   2. nine _____   3. zero _____   4. nineteen _____

5. fifty-nine _____   6. three hundred twenty-five _____

7. five hundred sixty thousand, forty nine   _____

8. nine hundred million, thirteen thousand, six   _____

Write the words for the following numbers.

9. 7 _____   10. 3 _____   11. 18 _____   12. 10 _____

13. 92 _____   14. 405 _____

15. 8,764 _____

16. 1,340,000 _____

Circle the numbers with

17. 7 in the ones place   18. 6 in the tens place   19. 4 in the ones place

   72 27 75 77   76 57 65 56   41 44 43 47

20. 9 in the hundreds place   21. 8 in the thousands place

   9,975 8,904 7,893 6,908 8,892   7,689 6,796 8,769 6,899 8,606

Circle the number that is in the ten thousands place.

22. 42,590   23. 503,732   24. 1,543,209   25. 759,601

Circle the number that is in the one millions place.

26. 32,456,790   **27.** 2,808,135   **28.** 9,888,452

Circle the numbers that are

29. < 9

     12   8   754   7

30. < 24

     14   69   23   345

31. > 350

     351   360   346

32. < 100

     999   99   101

33. < 1,000

     23   1,001   999

34. > 1,000

     23   1,001   999

Order the numbers from smallest to largest.

35. 1,020   1,021   1,121

    _____ _____ _____

36. 999   9,099   9,909

    _____ _____ _____

Round the number to the nearest

	thousand	hundred thousand	ten million
37. 665,565,665	_____	_____	_____

Round the number to the nearest

	million	ten thousand	hundred
38. 37,567,591	_____	_____	_____

Problem Solving

Solve the following problems.

39. The five baritones in the choir were asked to stand in order of their heights. Their heights were 69 inches, 72 inches, 65 inches, 60 inches, and 75 inches. Put them in order from shortest to tallest.

_____

40. Theo and Ed were arguing about who had spent more on detailing their trucks. Theo spent $390 and Ed spent $425. Who spent more?   _____

2

Addition and Subtraction Basic Facts

How many?

1.

_____ tennis balls

2.

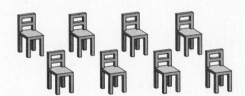

_____ chairs

Write the words or numbers.

3. 6 _____

4. 11 _____

5. ten _____

6. fourteen _____

Add.

7. 7 + 8 = _____

8. 2 + 4 = _____

9. 3 + 9 = _____

10. 8 + 8 = _____

11. $\begin{array}{r} 5 \\ + 8 \\ \hline \end{array}$

12. $\begin{array}{r} 7 \\ + 4 \\ \hline \end{array}$

13. $\begin{array}{r} 6 \\ + 0 \\ \hline \end{array}$

14. $\begin{array}{r} 9 \\ + 5 \\ \hline \end{array}$

15.
$$\begin{array}{r} 3\,0\,0 \\ +\,2\,0\,0 \\ \hline \end{array}$$

16.
$$\begin{array}{r} 7\,4 \\ +\,1\,2 \\ \hline \end{array}$$

17.
$$\begin{array}{r} 6\,4\,2 \\ +\,1\,2\,1 \\ \hline \end{array}$$

Subtract.

18. $12 - 9 = $ ___

19. $18 - 9 = $ ___

20. $15 - 7 = $ ___

21. $16 - 9 = $ ___

22. $58 - 10 = $ ___

23. $765 - 24 = $ ___

24. $599 - 201 = $ ___

25.
$$\begin{array}{r} 8\,4 \\ -\,4\,2 \\ \hline \end{array}$$

26.
$$\begin{array}{r} 9\,8\,5 \\ -\,8\,3\,1 \\ \hline \end{array}$$

27.
$$\begin{array}{r} 8\,3\,4 \\ -\,1\,0\,2 \\ \hline \end{array}$$

Problem Solving

Add or subtract to solve the following.

28. Mr. Dakatar bought a 5-pound chuck roast and 4 pounds of pork chops. How many pounds of meat did he buy in all?

_____

29. Harold typed 45 pages on Monday. He typed 34 pages on Tuesday. How many pages did he type in all?

_____

30. Mr. Swertlow had $896 in the bank. He took out $455. How much did he have left?

_____

31. Mrs. Diller's turkey weighed 16 pounds. There were 4 pounds left over after dinner. How many pounds of turkey were eaten?

_____

Write four different number sentences using: 8, 9, 17.

32. _____ _____ _____ _____

Finish these number sentences.

33. ___ $- 7 = 5$

34. $6 + $ ___ $= 15$

35. $13 - $ ___ $= 9$

36. $12 + $ ___ $= 20$

37. ___ $- 8 = 13$

38. ___ $+ 7 = 19$

Counting

Counting things is one way to use numbers. How many people are in each picture?

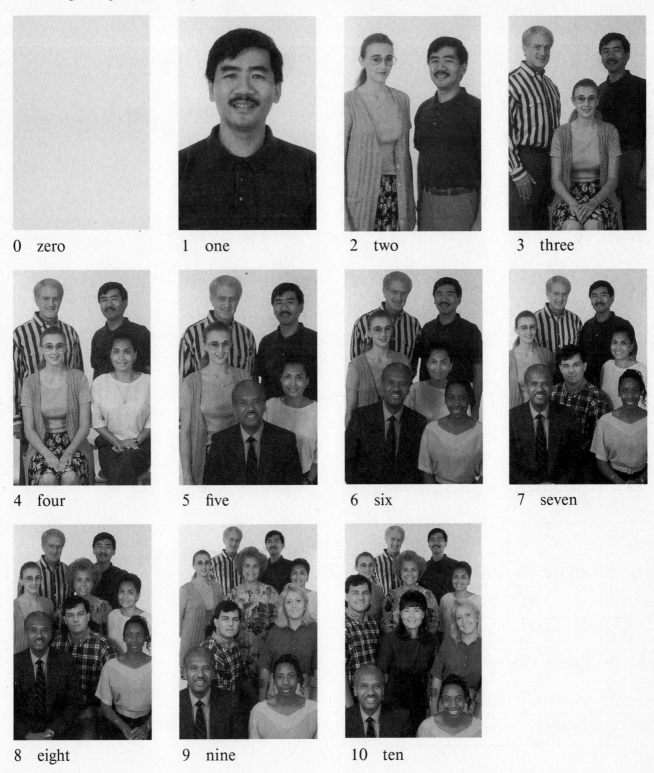

0   zero   1   one   2   two   3   three

4   four   5   five   6   six   7   seven

8   eight   9   nine   10   ten

27

How many people are in the picture? How many students?

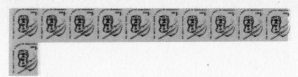

11 eleven

12 twelve

13 thirteen

14 fourteen

15 fifteen

16 sixteen

17 seventeen

18 eighteen

How many pennies are in line 10?

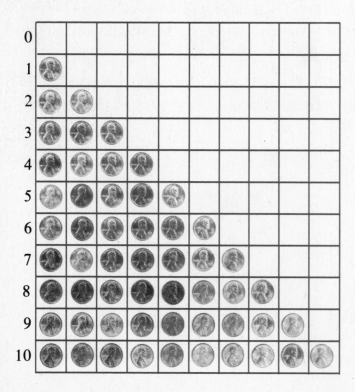

How many?

1.

$\underline{2}$
shoes

2.

_____
peanuts

3.

_____
keys

4.

_____
fish

5.

_____
balls

6.

_____
apples

Circle the number that tells the number of spots.

7.

1   2   3   4

8.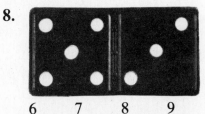

6   7   8   9

9.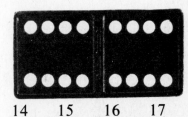

14   15   16   17

10.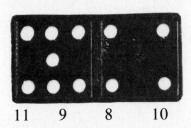

11   9   8   10

11.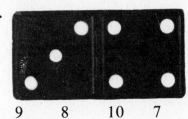

9   8   10   7

12.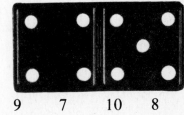

9   7   10   8

Write the numbers or words.

13. two $\underline{2}$ 14. zero   _____   15. sixteen   _____

16. eight   _____   17. eleven   _____   18. eighteen   _____

19. 3   _three_   20. 12   _____   21. 15   _____

LIFE SKILL

Writing the Time

It's 15 minutes after 4 o'clock.
Write the time this way.

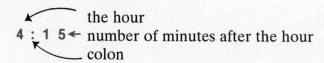

the hour
4 : 1 5 ← number of minutes after the hour
colon

Write two numbers after the colon even if the numbers are zero.

5:00
five o'clock

5:07
seven minutes after five

5:43
forty-three minutes
after five

Use a clock face like a number line to add or subtract hours.
To *add* hours, move *clockwise* around the clock. Clockwise is
the direction the clock hands move.
To *subtract* hours, move *counterclockwise*—the other way.

Later means to *add.*
Earlier means to *subtract.*

It's 11:35.
What time is 2 hours later?   1:35
What time is 3 hours earlier?   8:35

Earlier  Later

Write the time in numbers.

1. seven o'clock _____

2. two minutes after seven _____

3. twelve minutes after seven _____

4. thirty minutes after seven _____

London   Rio De Janeiro   Geneva   New York

Write the time in words.

5. 10:09 _____ **6.** 12:45 _____

7. 1:50 _____ **8.** 9:00 _____

9. It's 7:15 in Detroit. It's 3 hours earlier in Reno. What time
is it in Reno? _____

10. It's 9:30. You have to take a pill in 4 hours. When will you
take your next pill? _____

Addition Facts

To put together is to **add**.

Example

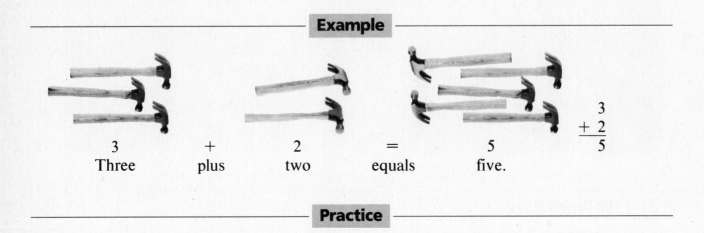

| 3 | + | 2 | = | 5 | $\begin{array}{r} 3 \\ + 2 \\ \hline 5 \end{array}$ |
| Three | plus | two | equals | five. | |

Practice

Write the number of items below each picture. Then write the problem again as shown above.

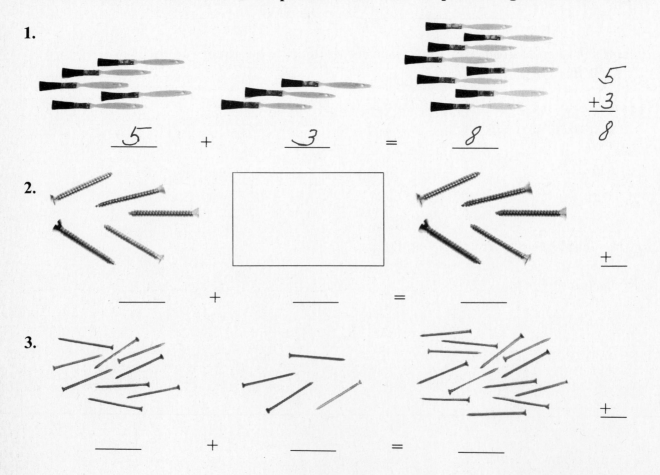

1.

_5_ + _3_ = _8_ $\begin{array}{r} 5 \\ +3 \\ \hline 8 \end{array}$

2.

___ + ___ = ___ $\begin{array}{r} \\ + \\ \hline \end{array}$

3.

___ + ___ = ___ $\begin{array}{r} \\ + \\ \hline \end{array}$

Number Lines—Addition

Number lines can be useful as an addition tool. A number line is shown below.

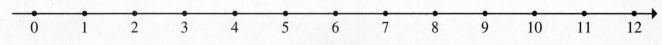

Examples

A. What is 3 added to 4?

A number line can help you add 3 to 4.

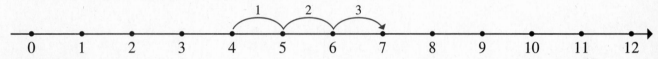

Start at 4.
Move 3 spaces to the right.
Moving to the right shows addition: 4 + 3 = 7.

B. What is 3 more than 8?
You can use a number
line to find the answer.
Start at 8.
Move 3 spaces to
   the right.
   8 + 3 = 11.
3 more than 8 = 11.

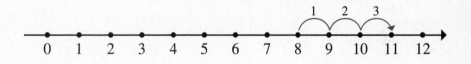

Practice

Use the number line to add these numbers.

1. 6 + 5 = _11_

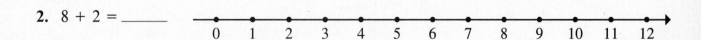

2. 8 + 2 = _____

3. $7 + 4 =$ _____

0   1   2   3   4   5   6   7   8   9   10   11   12

4. $3 + 8 =$ _____

0   1   2   3   4   5   6   7   8   9   10   11   12

5. $2 + 7 =$ _____

0   1   2   3   4   5   6   7   8   9   10   11   12

6. $3 + 5 =$ _____

0   1   2   3   4   5   6   7   8   9   10   11   12

7. $6 + 6 =$ _____

0   1   2   3   4   5   6   7   8   9   10   11   12

8. $5 + 5 =$ _____

0   1   2   3   4   5   6   7   8   9   10   11   12

9. $4 + 4 =$ _____

0   1   2   3   4   5   6   7   8   9   10   11   12

10. $4 + 6 =$ _____

0   1   2   3   4   5   6   7   8   9   10   11   12

Use the number line to find these answers.

11. What is 2 more than 4?

$4 + 2 =$ _6_

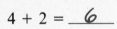

0   1   2   3   4   5   6   7   8   9   10   11   12

12. What is 5 more than 3?

$3 + 5 =$ _____

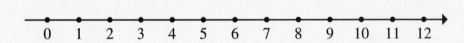

0   1   2   3   4   5   6   7   8   9   10   11   12

13. What is 4 more than 8?

$8 + 4 =$ _____

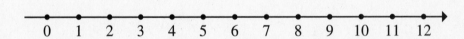

0   1   2   3   4   5   6   7   8   9   10   11   12

14. What is 5 more than 5?

$5 + 5 =$ _____

0   1   2   3   4   5   6   7   8   9   10   11   12

15. What is 2 more than 9?

$9 + 2 =$ _____

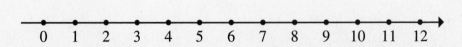

0   1   2   3   4   5   6   7   8   9   10   11   12

Add. Use a number line to help you.

16. $3 + 1 = $ ___   **17.** $2 + 2 = $ ___   **18.** $9 + 0 = $ ___   **19.** $8 + 8 = $ ___

20. $3 + 3 = $ ___   **21.** $6 + 0 = $ ___   **22.** $9 + 9 = $ ___   **23.** $4 + 4 = $ ___

24. $4 + 3 = $ ___   **25.** $9 + 1 = $ ___   **26.** $0 + 4 = $ ___   **27.** $2 + 0 = $ ___

28. $4 + 5 = $ ___   **29.** $1 + 8 = $ ___   **30.** $3 + 3 = $ ___   **31.** $0 + 1 = $ ___

32. $4 + 8 = $ ___   **33.** $0 + 7 = $ ___   **34.** $8 + 9 = $ ___   **35.** $7 + 5 = $ ___

36. $5 + 6 = $ ___   **37.** $7 + 7 = $ ___   **38.** $6 + 6 = $ ___   **39.** $8 + 5 = $ ___

40. $5 + 8 = $ ___   **41.** $0 + 3 = $ ___   **42.** $3 + 8 = $ ___   **43.** $6 + 9 = $ ___

Add.

44. $\begin{array}{r} 3 \\ + 6 \\ \hline \end{array}$ **45.** $\begin{array}{r} 4 \\ + 4 \\ \hline \end{array}$ **46.** $\begin{array}{r} 5 \\ + 3 \\ \hline \end{array}$ **47.** $\begin{array}{r} 6 \\ + 1 \\ \hline \end{array}$

48. $\begin{array}{r} 9 \\ + 5 \\ \hline \end{array}$ **49.** $\begin{array}{r} 7 \\ + 2 \\ \hline \end{array}$ **50.** $\begin{array}{r} 4 \\ + 6 \\ \hline \end{array}$ **51.** $\begin{array}{r} 0 \\ + 8 \\ \hline \end{array}$

52. $\begin{array}{r} 8 \\ + 9 \\ \hline \end{array}$ **53.** $\begin{array}{r} 8 \\ + 2 \\ \hline \end{array}$ **54.** $\begin{array}{r} 8 \\ + 1 \\ \hline \end{array}$ **55.** $\begin{array}{r} 1 \\ + 9 \\ \hline \end{array}$

Problem Solving

Solve these problems using addition and the number line to help you.

56. Ken spent $9 for holiday greeting cards and $4 for mailing them. How much did he spend? _____

57. There are nine short women and seven tall women. How many women are there in all? _____

58. Write your own addition word problem and solve it. _____

Simple Adding

The basic addition facts are also used to add larger numbers. Follow these steps:

Step 1   Write the first number.

Step 2   Write the second number under the first.

Step 3   Add each column, starting with the ones.

─────────────────────────── **Examples** ───────────────────────────

A. Add. 41 + 15 = ?

	Tens	Ones
Step 1	4	1
Step 2	+ 1	5
Step 3	5	6

1 + 5 = 6
4 + 1 = 5

MATH HINT

B̲e sure to line up the ones under the ones, the tens under the tens, and so on.

The answer has 5 tens and 6 ones.
The answer is 56.
41 + 15 = 56

Sum is another word for the answer in an addition problem.

B. Find this sum. 302 + 56 = _____

	Hundreds	Tens	Ones
Step 1	3	0	2
Step 2	+	5	6
Step 3	3	5	8

2 + 6 = 8
0 + 5 = 5
3 + 0 = 3

The answer has 3 hundreds, 5 tens, and 8 ones.
The answer is 358.
302 + 56 = 358

Find these sums.

1. $\begin{array}{r} 6\,0 \\ +\,2\,0 \\ \hline \end{array}$
2. $\begin{array}{r} 4\,0 \\ +\,3\,0 \\ \hline \end{array}$
3. $\begin{array}{r} 7\,0 \\ +\,1\,0 \\ \hline \end{array}$
4. $\begin{array}{r} 5\,0 \\ +\,4\,0 \\ \hline \end{array}$

5. $\begin{array}{r} 2\,0\,0 \\ +\,2\,0\,0 \\ \hline \end{array}$
6. $\begin{array}{r} 6\,0\,0 \\ +\,3\,0\,0 \\ \hline \end{array}$
7. $\begin{array}{r} 5\,0\,0 \\ +\,1\,0\,0 \\ \hline \end{array}$
8. $\begin{array}{r} 4\,0\,0 \\ +\,3\,0\,0 \\ \hline \end{array}$

9. $\begin{array}{r} 7\,6 \\ +\,1\,2 \\ \hline \end{array}$
10. $\begin{array}{r} 4\,2 \\ +\,1\,3 \\ \hline \end{array}$
11. $\begin{array}{r} 6\,1 \\ +\,2\,8 \\ \hline \end{array}$
12. $\begin{array}{r} 3\,5 \\ +\,2\,0 \\ \hline \end{array}$

13. $\begin{array}{r} 8\,0 \\ +\;\;\,3 \\ \hline \end{array}$
14. $\begin{array}{r} 2\,2 \\ +\;\;\,6 \\ \hline \end{array}$
15. $\begin{array}{r} 1\,1 \\ +\;\;\,8 \\ \hline \end{array}$
16. $\begin{array}{r} 8\,4 \\ +\;\;\,5 \\ \hline \end{array}$

17. $\begin{array}{r} 5\,5\,5 \\ +\,2\,2\,2 \\ \hline \end{array}$
18. $\begin{array}{r} 6\,0\,0 \\ +\,3\,4\,9 \\ \hline \end{array}$
19. $\begin{array}{r} 5\,0\,2 \\ +\,2\,7\,3 \\ \hline \end{array}$
20. $\begin{array}{r} 7\,1\,1 \\ +\,1\,0\,0 \\ \hline \end{array}$

21. $30 + 10 = $ _____
22. $42 + 3 = $ _____
23. $100 + 45 = $ _____

24. $234 + 123 = $ _____
25. $162 + 27 = $ _____
26. $978 + 11 = $ _____

27. $430 + 64 = $ _____
28. $207 + 42 = $ _____
29. $602 + 146 = $ _____

30. $123 + 456 = $ _____
31. $870 + 105 = $ _____
32. $168 + 421 = $ _____

Problem Solving—Addition

Remember how you solved word problems in Lesson 6. Use the following steps to help you:

Step 1   Read the problem and underline the key words. These words will generally relate to some computation.

Step 2   Make a plan to solve the problem. Ask yourself, Should I add, subtract, multiply, divide, round, or compare? You may have to do more than one of these operations for the same problem.

Step 3   Find the solution. Use your math knowledge to find your answer. Carry out the computation.

Step 4   Check the answer. Ask yourself, Is the answer reasonable? Did you find what you were asked for?

Here are some key words you should know for addition problems:

altogether	in all	total
both	sum	together
increase		

--- **Example** ---

You have three cans of red paint and seven cans of white paint. How many cans of paint do you have in all?

Follow these steps to solve this problem:

Step 1   The key words are **three cans of red paint, seven cans of white paint,** and **how many in all.**

Step 2   This problem requires you to **add** the number of cans of red paint and the cans of white paint.

Step 3 $3 + 7 = 10$ cans of paint

Step 4   You can use a number line to recheck your addition. Since you are adding, your total should be larger than 3 or 7.

Solve the following problems.

1. There is no one home. Maria arrives home. How many people are at home? _____

2. Three people vote **Yes** on the ballot. Nine people vote **No.** How many people voted altogether? _____

3. Leon has five boxes of cards. He gets two more boxes. What is the total number of boxes Leon has now? _____

4. Oscar had six dollars. He earned nine more. How many dollars does Oscar have now? _____

5. George packed three shirts with long sleeves and five shirts with short sleeves. How many shirts did he pack altogether? _____

6. Nine people came to the party on time. Six more people arrived late. How many people were at the party in all? _____

7. Brenda bought a skirt on sale for $9. She also bought shorts for $9. What is the sum of money she spent? _____

8. Mr. Tagashi worked 9 hours on Monday. He also worked 7 hours on Tuesday. How many hours did he work in all? _____

9. It is seven miles from Zach's house to his job. What is the total number of miles Zach must go to get back and forth to work? _____

10. Lucia's haircut cost $8 one month and $9 the next month. How much did she spend in all for haircuts? _____

11. Carlos works Monday through Friday. He earns $215 a week. Last week he also worked on Saturday and earned an additional $52. How much did Carlos earn last week? _____

12. Jenna took a car trip. She spent $37 for gas one way and $41 for gas on her return trip. How much did she spend altogether? _____

13. Kirby's bus fare was $60. His daughter's fare was $25. What was the total cost of the two bus fares? _____

14. Victor's car cost $12,645. The sales tax was $885. How much did Victor have to pay for the car altogether? _____

LIFE SKILL

Adding Change

These are the U.S. coins worth less than one dollar.

1¢	5¢	10¢	25¢	50¢

Coins are used together to make larger amounts.

Sue made calls from a pay phone. How much did each call cost?

1.
_____

2.
_____

3.
_____

4.
_____

5.
_____

6.
_____

Some people do their wash at a laundromat. Each washing machine costs $1.00—four quarters. Each dryer costs 75¢—3 quarters.

7. How many coins are needed to wash and dry one load?

_____

8. Mia washed three loads and used four dryers. How much money did she need?

_____

9. Calvin washed a load of towels. He put them through the dryer twice. How many coins did he use?

_____

10. Kareem washed and dried two loads of clothes. How much did it cost?

_____

Subtraction Facts

To take away is one way to **subtract**.

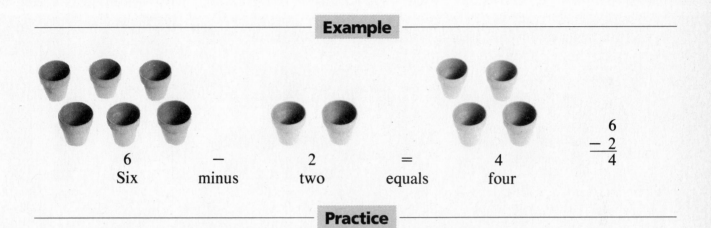

6	–	2	=	4	$\begin{array}{r} 6 \\ -2 \\ \hline 4 \end{array}$
Six	minus	two	equals	four	

Write the number of items below each picture. Then, rewrite the problem.

1.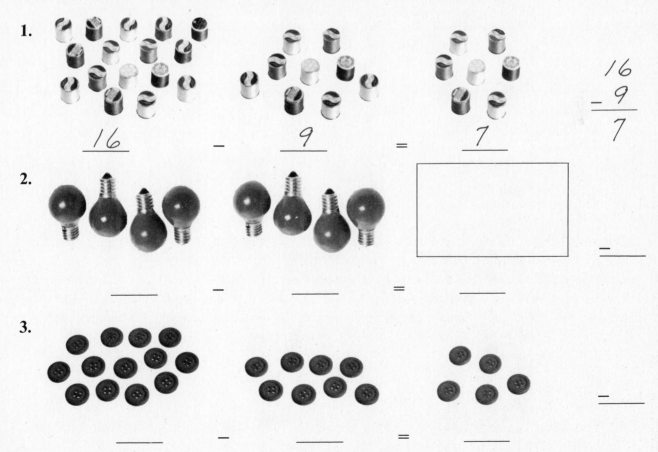

_16_ – _9_ = _7_ $\begin{array}{r} 16 \\ -9 \\ \hline 7 \end{array}$

2. ____ – ____ = ____ ⬜ $-$ ____

3. ____ – ____ = ____ ____

LIFE SKILL

Getting the Right Change

A. Paul has a dollar bill. He buys a note pad for 80¢. How much money should he get back?

Think:

Paul has   He spends    His change is

100¢   80¢   20¢

B. Louella has a quarter. She buys a postcard for 15¢. How much change should she get?

Think:

25¢ = 10¢ + 10¢ + 5¢

Louella has: She spends   Her change is

25¢   15¢   10¢

Find the amount of change.

1. You have   You spend   Your change is

50¢   15¢   _____

2. You have   You spend   Your change is

$1   25¢   _____

3. You have   You spend   Your change is

35¢   5¢   _____

4. You have   You spend   Your change is

$1   40¢   _____

Number Lines—Subtraction

Number lines can also help you subtract.

Examples

A. Subtract. $5 - 2 = ?$

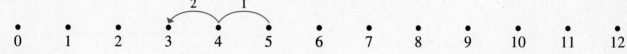

Start at 5.
Move 2 spaces to the left.
Moving to the left shows subtraction: $5 - 2 = 3$.

B. 6 is how many more than 4?

You can use a number line to find out.
Start at 6. Move to 4.
4 is 2 spaces to the left.

$$6 - 2 = 4$$

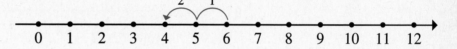

6 is 2 more than 4.

Practice

Use the number line to subtract these numbers.

1. $12 - 3 =$ _____

2. $10 - 8 =$ _____

3. $7 - 3 =$ _____

4. $8 - 5 =$ _____

5. $11 - 6 =$ _____

6. 12 − 9 = _____

0 1 2 3 4 5 6 7 8 9 10 11 12

7. 10 − 7 = _____

0 1 2 3 4 5 6 7 8 9 10 11 12

8. 9 − 4 = _____

0 1 2 3 4 5 6 7 8 9 10 11 12

9. 2 − 2 = _____

0 1 2 3 4 5 6 7 8 9 10 11 12

10. 10 − 3 = _____

0 1 2 3 4 5 6 7 8 9 10 11 12

11. 8 − 4 = _____

0 1 2 3 4 5 6 7 8 9 10 11 12

12. 3 − 2 = _____

0 1 2 3 4 5 6 7 8 9 10 11 12

Use the number line to find these answers.

13. 8 is how many more than 5?

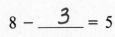 8 − _**3**_ = 5

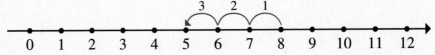

0 1 2 3 4 5 6 7 8 9 10 11 12

14. 11 is how many more than 7?

11 − _____ = 7

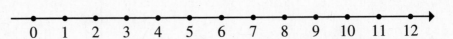

0 1 2 3 4 5 6 7 8 9 10 11 12

15. 6 is how many more than 1?

6 − _____ = 1

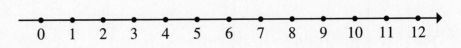

0 1 2 3 4 5 6 7 8 9 10 11 12

16. 12 is how many more than 9?

12 − _____ = 9

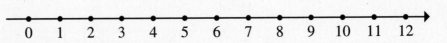

0 1 2 3 4 5 6 7 8 9 10 11 12

17. 9 is how many more than 4?

9 − _____ = 4

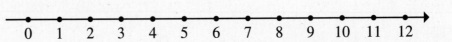

0 1 2 3 4 5 6 7 8 9 10 11 12

44

Subtract. Use a number line to help you.

18. $3 - 2 =$ _____   19. $5 - 2 =$ _____   20. $7 - 3 =$ _____

21. $9 - 8 =$ _____   22. $5 - 4 =$ _____   23. $6 - 3 =$ _____

24. $6 - 1 =$ _____   25. $8 - 4 =$ _____   26. $8 - 6 =$ _____

27. $9 - 2 =$ _____   28. $7 - 4 =$ _____   29. $2 - 1 =$ _____

30. $1 - 0 =$ _____   31. $4 - 1 =$ _____   32. $4 - 2 =$ _____

33. $7 - 7 =$ _____   34. $12 - 6 =$ _____   35. $13 - 9 =$ _____

Subtract.

36. $\begin{array}{r} 4 \\ -\ 1 \\ \hline \end{array}$ 37. $\begin{array}{r} 8 \\ -\ 0 \\ \hline \end{array}$ 38. $\begin{array}{r} 7 \\ -\ 6 \\ \hline \end{array}$

39. $\begin{array}{r} 1\ 0 \\ -\ 8 \\ \hline \end{array}$ 40. $\begin{array}{r} 1\ 6 \\ -\ 9 \\ \hline \end{array}$ 41. $\begin{array}{r} 1\ 2 \\ -\ 9 \\ \hline \end{array}$

42. $\begin{array}{r} 1\ 7 \\ -\ 8 \\ \hline \end{array}$ 43. $\begin{array}{r} 1\ 1 \\ -\ 8 \\ \hline \end{array}$ 44. $\begin{array}{r} 1\ 5 \\ -\ 7 \\ \hline \end{array}$

45. $\begin{array}{r} 1\ 3 \\ -\ 7 \\ \hline \end{array}$ 46. $\begin{array}{r} 1\ 2 \\ -\ 8 \\ \hline \end{array}$ 47. $\begin{array}{r} 1\ 0 \\ -\ 4 \\ \hline \end{array}$

Problem Solving

Solve these problems using subtraction.

48. There are five planes at the airport. One takes off. How many planes are left? _____

49. A car dealer sold fifteen cars. The dealer across the street sold six cars. How many more cars did the first dealer sell? _____

50. Eileen spent eleven dollars. Her sister spent five dollars. What is the difference in the amounts they spent? _____

51. Write your own subtraction word problem and solve it. _____

Simple Subtracting

To subtract numbers, follow these steps:

Step 1   Write the first number.

Step 2   Write the second number under the first.

Step 3   Subtract, starting with the ones column.

Examples

A. Subtract. 36 − 23 = _____

	Tens	Ones
Step 1	3	6
Step 2	− 2	3
Step 3	1	3

$$6 - 3 = 3$$
$$3 - 2 = 1$$

> **MATH HINT**
>
> **B**e sure to line up the ones under the ones, the tens under the tens.

The answer has 1 ten and 3 ones.
The answer is 13.
36 − 23 = 13

B. Roberta made $165 last week. She spent $63 on food. How much is left?

	Hundreds	Tens	Ones
Step 1	1	6	5
Step 2	−	6	3
Step 3	1	0	2

$$5 - 3 = 2$$
$$6 - 6 = 0$$
$$1 - 0 = 1$$

> **MATH HINT**
>
> **B**e sure to line up the ones, the tens, and the hundreds.

The answer has 1 hundred, 0 tens, and 2 ones.
The answer is 102.
165 − 63 = 102

Subtract.

1. 50
  −40

2. 90
  −60

3. 65
  −10

4. 78
  −14

5. 37
  −25

6. 87
  −74

7. 75
  − 2

8. 19
  − 8

9. 138
  − 17

10. 676
  − 41

11. 846
  − 12

12. 555
  − 3

13. 968
  − 24

14. 329
  − 15

15. 777
  −111

16. 585
  −300

17. 649 − 100 = _____

18. 395 − 202 = _____

19. 208 − 4 = _____

20. 296 − 55 = _____

21. 999 − 707 = _____

22. 711 − 601 = _____

23. 567 − 42 = _____

24. 407 − 107 = _____

25. 898 − 660 = _____

26. 340 − 20 = _____

27. 695 − 422 = _____

28. 478 − 2 = _____

29. 999 − 123 = _____

30. 505 − 101 = _____

31. 129 − 19 = _____

Problem Solving—Subtraction

You have already been introduced to the problem-solving steps. Those steps are:

Step 1 Read the problem and underline the key words. These words will usually relate to some mathematics reasoning computation.

Step 2 Make a plan to solve the problem. Ask yourself, Should I add, subtract, multiply, divide, round, or compare? You may have to do more than one of these operations for the same problem.

Step 3 Find the solution. Use your math knowledge to find your answer.

Step 4 Check the answer. Ask yourself, Is the answer reasonable? Did you find what you were asked for?

Here are some key words you should know for subtraction problems:

decreased by	difference	remainder
diminished by	how much less	how much more
	how many left	how many fewer

Example

You have eight dollars. You spend two dollars. How many dollars do you have left?

Step 1 Determine how many dollars you have left. The key words are **how many left.**

Step 2 The key word indicates which operation should occur—subtraction. You will subtract the number of dollars you spent from the number of dollars you started with.

Step 3 Find the solution.
$8 - 2 = 6$.

Step 4 Check the answer. You can use a number line or recheck your subtraction. If you move 8 spaces on the number line and then go back 2, you are at 6. Therefore, your answer is correct.

Solve the following problems.

1. You have $13. You spend $7. How many dollars do you have left? _____

2. One class has 13 students. Another class has 8 students. What is the difference in the number of students? _____

3. There are 16 questions on the test. You have no wrong answers. How many right answers do you have? _____

4. Lee has 2 children. Hank has 6 children. How many more children does Hank have? _____

5. Cliff worked 9 hours. Toni worked 17 hours. How many fewer hours did Cliff work? _____

6. You need a new part for your car. You have $9. The part costs $15. How much more do you need? _____

7. Sheets cost $16 each at Smith Brothers. The same sheets cost $11 each at Giant Savers. What is the difference in price? _____

8. Carly's gas bill was $14 in January. It was $7 in September. How much less was her September bill? _____

9. Workers at the Bremen Company make $9 an hour. Workers at the City Plant make $7 an hour. How much less do the City Plant workers make? _____

10. Mr. Emshoff ran 7 miles a week in May and 10 miles a week in June. How many more miles a week did he run in June?

_____

11. Holly made $32 in tips. She gave $10 to the busboys. What did she take home?

_____

12. Mr. Ehrett weighs 167 pounds. He wants to weigh 150. How many pounds does he have to lose?

_____

13. A plane ticket to Elliottville costs $149. A train ticket is $42 less. How much is a train ticket?

_____

14. Eugene makes $85 a week. Lisa makes $60 a week. How much more a week does Eugene make than Lisa?

_____

15. The chapter 5 test had 45 questions on it, and the chapter 6 test had 55 questions on it. How many more questions did the chapter 6 test have?

_____

16. Last month it cost Arlene $359 to fly to Florida. This month it will cost her $245. How much is she saving if she flies this month?

_____

17. Duncan has been watching for a sale on a stereo he wants to buy. The stereo normally costs $999. Today's paper says it is on sale for $949. How much will he save if he buys it now?

_____

Number Sentences

This is a **number sentence:** $5 + 3 = 8$.
There are three other number sentences you can write using 5, 3, and 8. These four sentences using addition and subtraction are called a **family of facts.**

--------------------------------- Example ---------------------------------

$5 + 3 = 8$ $3 + 5 = 8$ $8 - 5 = 3$ $8 - 3 = 5$

--------------------------------- Practice ---------------------------------

Complete these number sentences. Each group of sentences is a family of facts.

1. $8 + 2 = $ _10_

    $2 + 8 = $ _____

    $10 - 2 = $ _____

    $10 - 8 = $ _____

2. $4 + 3 = $ _____

    $3 + 4 = $ _____

    $7 - 4 = $ _____

    $7 - 3 = $ _____

3. $6 + 9 = $ _____

    $9 + 6 = $ _____

    $15 - 9 = $ _____

    $15 - 6 = $ _____

4. $6 + 5 = $ _____

    $5 + 6 = $ _____

    $11 - 6 = $ _____

    $11 - 5 = $ _____

5. $8 + 7 = $ _____

    $7 + 8 = $ _____

    $15 - 8 = $ _____

    $15 - 7 = $ _____

6. $8 + 0 = $ _____

    $0 + 8 = $ _____

    $8 - 0 = $ _____

    $8 - 8 = $ _____

7. $7 + $ _5_ $ = 12$

    $5 + 7 = $ _____

    $12 - 7 = $ _____

    $12 - $ _____ $ = 7$

8. $1 + $ _____ $ = 9$

    $8 + $ _____ $ = 9$

    $9 - 1 = $ _____

    $9 - $ _____ $ = 1$

9. _____ $ + 3 = 10$

    $10 - 7 = $ _____

    $3 + 7 = $ _____

    $10 - 3 = $ _____

Write four number sentences for each group of numbers.

10. 6, 1, 7

_____ $6 + 1 = 7$ _____

_____

_____

_____

11. 8, 4, 12

_____

_____

_____

_____

12. 11, 7, 4

_____

_____

_____

_____

13. 15, 7, 8

_____

_____

_____

_____

14. 10, 2, 8

_____

_____

_____

_____

15. 6, 7, 13

_____

_____

_____

_____

16. 2, 5, 7

_____

_____

_____

_____

17. 3, 6, 9

_____

_____

_____

_____

18. 9, 0, 9 (See Practice #6.)

_____

_____

_____

_____

Fill in the missing numbers.

19. __6__ + 7 = 13

20. _____ + 6 = 11

21. 0 + _____ = 0

22. _____ + 7 = 14

23. _____ + 5 = 12

24. 10 − _____ = 5

25. _____ + 3 = 4

26. _____ + 9 = 11

27. 12 − _____ = 9

28. _____ + 9 = 10

29. _____ + 8 = 17

30. 2 + _____ = 10

31. 10 − _____ = 4

32. _____ + 4 = 13

33. 17 − _____ = 9

34. 1 − _____ = 0

35. _____ − 3 = 12

36. 13 + _____ = 13

Using an Addition Table

This is an **addition table.** The numbers above and to the left of the double lines are the numbers that are added. The numbers inside the squares are the answers.

The row for 2 and the column for 3 cross at 5.
This means that 3 + 2 = 5.
It also means that 2 + 3 = 5.
It also means that 5 − 3 = 2 and 5 − 2 = 3.

Finish the table to show all the basic addition facts. Then use the table to answer the questions that follow.

+	0	1	2	3	4	5	6	7	8	9
0	0	1	2	3						
1	1	2	3	4						
2	2	3	4	5						
3	3	4	5	6						
4						10				
5										14
6										
7										
8								15		
9				13						

1. The table shows three different ways to get 2 for an answer. What are they?

_____ + _____ = 2   _____ + _____ = 2   _____ + _____ = 2

2. The table shows that $1 + 2 = 3$. Use the table to find these answers.

$3 - 2 =$ _____ $3 - 1 =$ _____ $3 -$ _____ $= 2$ $3 -$ _____ $= 1$

Use the addition table to find the answers.

3. $2 + 4 =$ __6__

4. $3 + 4 =$ _____

5. $3 + 5 =$ _____

6. $3 + 6 =$ _____

7. $3 + 7 =$ _____

8. $3 + 8 =$ _____

9. $7 +$ _____ $= 7$

10. $7 +$ _____ $= 8$

11. $7 +$ _____ $= 9$

12. $7 +$ _____ $= 10$

13. $7 +$ _____ $= 11$

14. $7 +$ _____ $= 12$

15. $9 +$ _____ $= 12$

16. $12 -$ _____ $= 3$

17. $12 -$ _____ $= 9$

18. $5 +$ _____ $= 11$

19. $11 -$ _____ $= 5$

20. $11 -$ _____ $= 6$

21. $6 +$ _____ $= 13$

22. $13 -$ _____ $= 6$

23. $13 -$ _____ $= 7$

Fill in the missing + or − in these number sentences.

24. 4 __+__ $8 = 12$

25. 9 _____ $9 = 0$

26. 1 _____ $3 = 4$

27. 9 _____ $8 = 1$

28. 4 _____ $5 = 9$

29. 5 _____ $4 = 9$

30. 5 _____ $4 = 1$

31. 6 _____ $6 = 12$

32. 6 _____ $6 = 0$

33. 0 _____ $1 = 1$

34. 1 _____ $1 = 0$

35. 8 _____ $5 = 3$

36. 9 _____ $6 = 15$

37. 12 _____ $3 = 9$

38. 18 _____ $9 = 9$

Write two subtraction sentences for each addition sentence.

39. $3 + 6 = 9$ _____ $9 - 6 = 3$ _____   _____ $9 - 3 = 6$ _____

40. $9 + 3 = 12$ _____   _____

41. $5 + 6 = 11$ _____   _____

How many items in each figure?

1.

_____ birds

2.

_____ flowers

Write the words or numbers.

3. 9 _____   **4.** 14 _____   **5.** 8 _____   **6.** 12 _____

7. Eleven _____   **8.** Three _____   **9.** One _____   **10.** Sixteen _____

Add.

11. 8 + 4 = _____   **12.** 9 + 7 = _____   **13.** 6 + 4 = _____   **14.** 7 + 8 = _____

15. 7
       + 5

16. 2
       + 9

17. 8
       + 6

18. 9
       + 9

19. 30 + 60 = _____   **20.** 56 + 21 = _____   **21.** 304 + 215 = _____

22. 5 0
       + 2 0

23. 3 0
       + 1 4

24. 4 7 4
       + 2 1 3

25. 6 6 6
       +   3 3

Subtract.

26. $17 - 9 =$ _6_ **27.** $13 - 8 =$ ____ **28.** $12 - 3 =$ ____ **29.** $15 - 9 =$ ____

30. $\begin{array}{r} 1\ 1 \\ -\ 7 \\ \hline \end{array}$ **31.** $\begin{array}{r} 1\ 4 \\ -\ 9 \\ \hline \end{array}$ **32.** $\begin{array}{r} 1\ 0 \\ -\ 2 \\ \hline \end{array}$ **33.** $\begin{array}{r} 1\ 4 \\ -\ 8 \\ \hline \end{array}$

34. $47 - 11 =$ ____   **35.** $866 - 333 =$ ____   **36.** $294 - 181 =$ ____

37. $\begin{array}{r} 5\ 0 \\ -2\ 0 \\ \hline \end{array}$ **38.** $\begin{array}{r} 9\ 6 \\ -5\ 4 \\ \hline \end{array}$ **39.** $\begin{array}{r} 4\ 8\ 9 \\ -2\ 7\ 4 \\ \hline \end{array}$ **40.** $\begin{array}{r} 4\ 0\ 6 \\ -2\ 0\ 1 \\ \hline \end{array}$

Problem Solving

Add or subtract to solve the following.

41. The Sneeds have two cats and three dogs. How many pets do they have?

_____

42. A deli has 23 pounds of ham and 35 pounds of bread. How many pounds of food is this?

_____

43. There were 18 cookies. Raj ate 4. How many were left?

_____

44. Hank owed Arturo $35 for a concert ticket. He gave him a twenty-dollar bill. How much does he still owe Arturo?

_____

Write four different number sentences using 6, 5, 11.

45. _____   _____   _____   _____

Finish these number sentences.

46. ____ $+ 7 = 12$ **47.** $9 -$ ____ $= 6$ **48.** $8 +$ ____ $= 10$ **49.** ____ $- 7 = 4$

56

3
Addition

Find the sums.

1. 8 + 4 = _____   **2.** 6 + 6 = _____   **3.** 9 + 0 = _____   **4.** 9 + 5 = _____

5.   32   **6.**   79   **7.**   95   **8.**   87
      + 4 9   + 1 9   + 7 8   + 6 6

9.   2 9 3   **10.**   4 1 4   **11.**   3 8 9   **12.**   4 6 8
      +   7 6   +   3 6   + 2 0 4   + 2 0 2

13.   3 0 9   **14.**   7 8 7   **15.**   1 , 0 2 7   **16.**   5 , 6 7 8
      + 4 4 4   + 9 5 9   +   9 9 9   + 8 , 9 7 6

17.   7 8   **18.**   5 0 9   **19.**   1 , 9 5 5   **20.**   2 , 3 7 5
      + 1 7   + 2 3 7   + 2 , 8 1 1   + 1 , 2 8 2

21.
```
   89
 +77
```

22.
```
  666
 +508
```

23.
```
  8,402
 +1,999
```

24.
```
  5,934
 +1,876
```

25.
```
   24
   31
 +42
```

26.
```
  604
  113
 + 65
```

27.
```
  4,906
    817
 +1,659
```

28.
```
  7,190
  3,446
 +8,912
```

29. 675 + 43 + 289 + 1,034 =

30. 467 + 490 + 3,025 + 12 =

_____   _____

Problem Solving

Solve the following problems.

31. A shirt costs $23. A tie costs $9. How much do they cost
together?   _____

32. Jules had $569 in the bank. A relative left him $1,255. How
much does Jules have now?   _____

33. The Super Store had 1,098 large bags, 2,743 medium bags, and
576 small bags. It also had 102 extra-large bags. How many
bags did it have altogether?   _____

**For problems 34 and 35, estimate the answer to the nearest
thousand. Then find the exact answer.**

34.
```
    34,506
    12,788
 +108,155
```
Estimate: Exact:

_____   _____

35.
```
  356,789
 +107,555
```
Estimate: Exact:

_____   _____

36. A movie star raised $274,876 for sick children one year. She
raised $441,800 the next year. She raised $338,096 the third
year. How much did she raise in all? Estimate to the nearest ten
thousand.   _____

Addition With One Renaming

When working in addition, you must remember your place values and follow these steps:

Step 1 Add the numbers in the ones place.

Step 2 Now add the numbers in the tens column.

Step 3 Add the numbers in the hundreds column.

Step 4 Continue until there are no numbers left to combine.

Example

Add. 157 + 138 = ?   The answer is

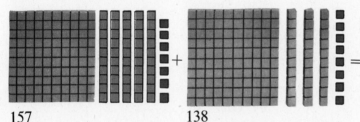   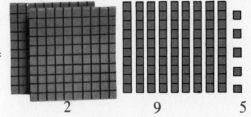

157   138   2   9   5

This is **renaming:** 7 ones + 8 ones = 15 ones

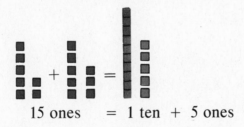

15 ones   = 1 ten + 5 ones

Step 1 7 + 8 = 15. Rename 15.
15 = 1 ten + 5 ones

$$\begin{array}{r} \overset{1}{1}57 \\ +138 \\ \hline 295 \end{array}$$

Put 5 ones in the ones place in the answer. ⟶
Put 1 ten above the tens column.

Step 2 1 + 5 + 3 = 9 (tens column) ⟶

Step 3 1 + 1 = 2 (hundreds column) ⟶

The answer has 2 hundreds + 9 tens + 5 ones. The answer is 295.

Find the sums.

1. $\begin{array}{r} 40 \\ +78 \end{array}$ 2. $\begin{array}{r} 36 \\ +91 \end{array}$ 3. $\begin{array}{r} 54 \\ +83 \end{array}$ 4. $\begin{array}{r} 66 \\ +92 \end{array}$

5. $\begin{array}{r} 105 \\ +\ \ 38 \end{array}$ 6. $\begin{array}{r} 943 \\ +\ \ 37 \end{array}$ 7. $\begin{array}{r} 455 \\ +162 \end{array}$ 8. $\begin{array}{r} 639 \\ +105 \end{array}$

Problem Solving

Solve the following problems.

9. A team scored 64 points in one game and 28 points in the next. How many total points did they score? _____

10. Juan has $129. Carlos has $38. How much money do they have together? _____

11. It cost Gerry $24 to rent a car. She spent $12 for gas. How much was her total cost? _____

12. Gloria drove 46 miles to Dallas. Then she drove 28 miles home. How many miles did she drive in all? _____

13. The doctor charged $135. The charge for X-rays was $95. How much was the total bill? _____

Addition With More Than One Renaming

When working in addition, line up the numbers in each place value position and remember to follow these steps:

Step 1 Add the numbers in the ones place.

Step 2 Add the numbers in the tens column.

Step 3 Add the numbers in the hundreds column.

Step 4 Add the numbers in the thousands column; continue until there are no numbers left to combine.

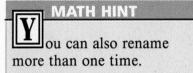
MATH HINT

You can also rename more than one time.

Example

Add. 1,429 + 1,863 = ?

Step 1 9 + 3 = 12 Rename 12.
12 = 1 ten + 2 ones.

Put 2 ones in the ones place in the answer.
Put 1 ten above the tens column.

Step 2 1 + 2 + 6 = 9 (tens column)

Step 3 4 + 8 = 12 Rename 12 hundreds.
12 hundreds = 1 thousand + 2 hundreds.

Put 2 hundreds in the hundreds place in the answer.
Put 1 thousand above the thousands column.

Step 4 1 + 1 + 1 = 3 (thousands column)

Write the numbers this way.

$$
\begin{array}{r}
1,4\overset{1}{2}9 \\
+1,863 \\
\hline
2
\end{array}
$$

$$
\begin{array}{r}
1,4\overset{1}{2}9 \\
+1,863 \\
\hline
92
\end{array}
$$

$$
\begin{array}{r}
\overset{1}{1},4\overset{1}{2}9 \\
+1,863 \\
\hline
292
\end{array}
$$

$$
\begin{array}{r}
\overset{1}{1},4\overset{1}{2}9 \\
+1,863 \\
\hline
3,292
\end{array}
$$

The answer has 3 thousands + 2 hundreds + 9 tens + 2 ones.
The answer is 3,292.

Add.

1. 908
   +117

2. 820
   +694

3. 603
   +599

4. 897
   +450

5. 777
   +349

6. 748
   +682

7. 895
   +399

8. 736
   +747

9. 1,479
   +2,843

10. 4,852
   + 989

11. 5,396
   +1,897

12. 7,463
   +1,999

13. 8,734
   + 878

14. 2,598
   +1,862

15. 6,981
   +1,749

16. 2,543
   +1,969

Solve the following problems.

17. Mirko pays $255 a month for rent. He pays $295 a month for food. How much does he spend on food and rent each month? _____

18. Gary spent $299 on his trip. Joyce spent $245. How much did the two spend together? _____

19. Ms. Hansen makes $188 a week. She worked last weekend for $56 more. How much were her total earnings? _____

20. Frank Klein drove to work every day. His yearly gas cost $787. Frank's wife took the train. A year's tickets came to $559. What did the Kleins spend in all to get to work? _____

21. Mr. Chen bought a car for $4,250. He paid $610 for car insurance. What did he spend for the car and the insurance? _____

22. The Hutzelmans put $13,450 down on a house. They paid a lawyer $1,570. What did they spend on the house and lawyer together? _____

23. Roxanne pays $3,460 a year for rent. She spends $3,780 a year for food. What does she spend on food and rent together? _____

24. Last year, Louis earned $18,800 teaching school. His summer job paid $2,623. What were his total earnings? _____

25. A band played for two nights. On Friday, 1,874 people attended the concert. On Saturday, 1,987 people came. How many people attended altogether? _____

26. Mr. Giles drove his truck 578 miles one week. He drove 652 miles the next week. How many miles did he drive both weeks? _____

27. Jaime paid $1,207 in taxes last year. This year he paid $934. How much were his taxes altogether? _____

Adding Three or More Numbers

Three or more numbers can be added together. They can be added in any order following the steps you have previously learned.

$$3 + 2 + 1 = 6$$
$$2 + 1 + 3 = 6$$
$$1 + 2 + 3 = 6$$

Example

Find the sum of 197 + 28 + 806 + 55.

Step 1
Write the numbers this way. Line them up by place value.

```
  1 9 7
    2 8
  8 0 6
    5 5
```

Step 2
Add the ones.
$7 + 8 = 15$
$15 + 6 = 21$
$21 + 5 = 26$

```
    ²
  1 9 7
    2 8
  8 0 6
    5 5
  _____
        6
```

Step 3
Add the tens.
$2 + 9 = 11$
$11 + 2 = 13$
$13 + 5 = 18$

```
  ¹ ²
  1 9 7
    2 8
  8 0 6
    5 5
  _____
      8 6
```

Step 4
Add the hundreds.
$1 + 1 = 2$
$2 + 8 = 10$

```
  ¹ ²
  1 9 7
    2 8
  8 0 6
    5 5
  _____
  1 , 0 8 6
```

Practice

Add.

1.
```
    2
    4
    6
  + 8
```

2.
```
    9
    8
    7
  + 6
```

3.
```
    6
    6
    5
  + 4
```

4.
```
    8
    9
    2
  + 7
```

5.
```
   2 1
   6 8
 + 3 7
```

6.
```
   5 5
   4 6
 + 9 8
```

7.
```
   6 9
   9 8
 + 7 6
```

8.
```
   8 8
   9 9
 + 5 5
```

9.
```
  1,102
      5
     41
+   100
```

10.
```
  2,395
    195
    843
+    27
```

11.
```
  3,408
      6
    677
+    72
```

12.
```
     96
  4,570
    209
+    21
```

13.
```
  302
  697
+513
```

14.
```
  499
  560
+382
```

15.
```
  632
   19
+  97
```

16.
```
  854
  907
+  81
```

17.
```
  1,107
    357
+   943
```

18.
```
  3,596
  1,234
+   902
```

19.
```
  2,560
  1,683
+2,119
```

20.
```
  4,739
  2,730
+1,141
```

21.
```
  2,589
      4
     23
+   972
```

22.
```
    578
  1,423
    666
+3,002
```

23.
```
  5,009
  1,860
      5
+   643
```

24.
```
      7
  4,053
     29
+   347
```

Line up these numbers by place value. Then add.

25. 34 + 578 + 65 + 1,009 =

_____
_____
_____
+ _____

26. 4 + 583 + 90 + 17 =

_____
_____
_____
+ _____

27. 1,784 + 331 + 19 =

_____
_____
+ _____

28. 1,595 + 56 + 780 =

_____
_____
+ _____

LIFE SKILL

Using a Map

Road maps show where roads go, the number of miles between towns, and where roads cross.

Look at this map. Highways 193 and 14 cross in the middle. From there along 14 to Portwine is 5 miles. From Portwine south to Highway 58 is 9 miles. 9 + 5 = 14. There are 14 miles of Highway 14 between 58 and 193.

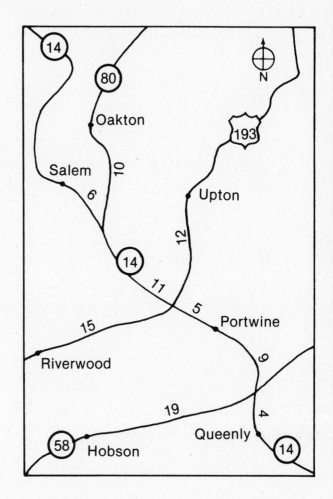

Use the map to answer these questions.

1. How many miles of Highway 14 between Salem and Portwine?

    _____

2. You are driving from Queenly to Hobson. You take Route 14 to Route 58. How far is it from Queenly to Hobson?

    _____

3. How far is it on Highway 193 from Upton to Route 14?

    _____

4. How many miles is it from Oakton to Queenly?

    _____

5. How many miles on 193 from Riverwood to Upton?

    _____

6. Find a map with your city on it. If you drive for 50 miles, where could you go?

    _____

66

Adding Large Numbers

Add large numbers the same way you add small numbers. Line up the digits by place value. Add from right to left.

Examples

A. Add.

$$\begin{array}{r} \overset{1}{5}6,732 \\ +70,910 \\ \hline 127,642 \end{array}$$

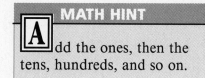

MATH HINT

Add the ones, then the tens, hundreds, and so on.

B. Many people watched TV one evening. 4,600 people watched Channel 11. 192,040 people watched Channel 5. 28,736 people watched Channel 9. 1,762,398 people watched Channel 12. How many people watched in all?

$$\begin{array}{r} \overset{1}{}\overset{1}{}\overset{1}{}\overset{1}{}\overset{1}{} \\ 4,600 \\ 192,040 \\ 28,736 \\ +1,762,398 \\ \hline 1,987,774 \ \text{people} \end{array}$$

Practice

Add.

1.
$$\begin{array}{r} 94,670 \\ +8,910 \\ \hline \end{array}$$

2.
$$\begin{array}{r} 364,591 \\ +158,993 \\ \hline \end{array}$$

3.
$$\begin{array}{r} 895,480 \\ +976,415 \\ \hline \end{array}$$

4.
$$\begin{array}{r} 10,569 \\ +8,983 \\ \hline \end{array}$$

5.
$$\begin{array}{r} 450,892 \\ +119,738 \\ \hline \end{array}$$

6.
$$\begin{array}{r} 667,485 \\ +223,846 \\ \hline \end{array}$$

7. 850,425 + 75,775 =

_____

8. 336,948 + 946,803 =

_____

9.
```
  6,903,452
     90,675
+ 8,134,983
```

10.
```
  903,472
    4,378
+ 891,413
```

11.
```
  1,345,921
+ 2,334,889
```

12. 41,237 + 12,999 + 8,001 =

_____

13. 3,289,873 + 444,555 + 319,009 =

_____

───────────────── **Problem Solving** ─────────────────

Solve the following problems.

14. Victor's house cost $112,645. The closing costs were $2,885. How much did the house cost?

_____

15. Tuition cost for Felix to go to college for one year was $18,695. His books cost $965; his room and board was $4,983. How much were the total costs for him to go to college for one year?

_____

16. Cal earns $14,456 a year. His sister earns $17,879. How much do both of them earn?

_____

17. The band sold 23,789 copies of its first record. It sold 92,631 copies of its second record. It sold 897,463 copies of its third record. How many records did the band sell altogether?

_____

LIFE SKILL

Making a Budget

Mr. and Mrs. Torrez kept a record of their income and expenses for a month. Find their weekly and monthly totals.

Income	Mrs. Torrez	Mr. Torrez	Weekly Income	Monthly bills	
Week 1	$276	$352	1. _____	Telephone	$ 28
				Rent	455
Week 2	295	352	2. _____	Gas	89
				Electricity	65
Week 3	257	352	3. _____	Car payment	285
				Insurance	74
Week 4	376	402	4. _____		
				Total	
Total Income			5. _____	Monthly Bills	6. _____

Weekly expenses	Week 1	Week 2	Week 3	Week 4	Weekly Expenses
Groceries	$96	$82	$94	$105	7. _____
Transportation	31	34	28	32	8. _____
Clothing	86	32	54	11	9. _____
Entertainment	29	30	45	35	10. _____
Miscellaneous	56	65	52	61	11. _____
Laundry	18	29	18	10	12. _____
Day care	95	85	95	95	13. _____
Total weekly expenses					14. _____
Total monthly bills and weekly expenses					15. _____

Keep a record of your own income and expenses for one month.

Problem Solving—Estimating in Addition

Word problems can be mastered by following these steps:

Step 1 Read the problem and underline the key words. These words will usually relate to some mathematics reasoning computation.

Step 2 Make a plan to solve the problem. Ask yourself, Should I add, subtract, multiply, divide, round, or compare? You may have to do more than one of these operations for the same problem.

Step 3 Find the solution. Use your math knowledge.

Step 4 Check the answer. Ask yourself, Is the answer reasonable? Did you find what you were asked for?

The last step asks you to check the answer. Sometimes an estimate can be used to check if your answer is reasonable. You can estimate the answer by rounding to one of the place value positions. This means you must find that place value in the numbers you are working with and round up or down.

To estimate the answers in addition, remember these rules for rounding:
    If the number is 5 or greater, round up.
    If the number is less than 5, round down.

Example

Last year, the Conrad family spent $3,739 on meals eaten at home. They spent $2,056 on meals eaten out. How much did they spend on food altogether?

Step 1 Determine how much they spent on food altogether. The key word is **altogether.**

Step 2 The key word indicates which operation should occur—addition.

Step 3 Find the solution.
$$\begin{array}{r} \$3,739 \\ +2,056 \\ \hline \$5,795 \end{array}\quad \text{Total amount spent on food}$$

Step 4 Check the answer. Does it make sense that $3,739 + $2,056 = $5,795? Yes, the answer is reasonable.

Remember, you could check your answer by using estimation. Let's round these numbers to the nearest hundred to check your answer.

Exact

		Estimate
$3,739	3 is less than 5, so round down	3,700
+ 2,056	5 is rounded up	+2,100
$5,795	9 is greater than 5, so round up	5,800

Both the estimate and exact answers are reasonable.

─────────────────────────── **Practice** ───────────────────────────

Solve the following problems by estimating. Then give the exact answer.

1. Sondra bought a new television for $79 and a VCR for $125. Estimate how much she paid altogether for these two items. (Round to the nearest ten.)

    _____

    _____

2. The Community Park Group planted 133 trees, 247 bushes, and 119 flower beds this spring. Estimate how much they planted in all. (Round to the nearest ten.)

    _____

    _____

3. Centerberg has two high schools. The population of North High School is 1,453 students and the population of South High School is 849. Estimate the total high school population in Centerberg. (Round to the nearest ten)

    _____

    _____

4. When Jorge paid his taxes this year, he paid $2,690 to the federal government and $1,205 to the state. Estimate how much he paid altogether. (Round to the nearest hundred)

    _____

    _____

5. Beatriz earns $25,499 a year working for a law firm. Her husband makes $31,965 a year working as a roofer. Estimate their total income for this year. (Round to the nearest thousand)

    _____

    _____

LIFE SKILL

Counting Calories

Karen carefully watches what she eats. Find the calories for breakfast, lunch, and dinner. Find the total calories for each day.

Saturday

Breakfast	Calories
2 fried eggs	210
raisin toast with butter	150
coffee	0
orange juice	110
Breakfast total	_____

Lunch	
hamburger patty	275
1 carrot	20
cottage cheese	100
skim milk	88
Lunch total	_____

Dinner	
1 pork chop	290
broccoli	29
baked potato with yogurt	190
coffee	0
Dinner total	_____

Saturday total _____

Sunday

Breakfast	Calories
2 strips turkey bacon	100
$\frac{1}{2}$ grapefruit	70
1 pancake	75
coffee	0
Breakfast total	_____

Lunch	
chicken sandwich	260
skim milk	88
1 orange	75
Lunch total	_____

Dinner	
2 slices roast chicken	300
rice	100
cauliflower	33
spinach	23
coffee	0
Dinner total	_____

Sunday total _____

How many calories did Karen eat in all over the weekend? _____

Posttest

Find the sums.

1. 9 + 5 = _____

2. 8 + 8 = _____

3. 3 + 7 = _____

4. 0 + 5 = _____

5.
```
   23
 + 56
```

6.
```
   70
 + 18
```

7.
```
  123
 +566
```

8.
```
  508
 +461
```

9.
```
   88
 +  9
```

10.
```
   44
 + 27
```

11.
```
   38
 + 94
```

12.
```
   47
 + 79
```

13.
```
  406
 +267
```

14.
```
  578
 +255
```

15.
```
  843
 +409
```

16.
```
  591
 +879
```

17.
```
  2,930
 +1,835
```

18.
```
  5,739
 +1,806
```

19.
```
  8,805
 +7,618
```

20.
```
  5,914
 +8,398
```

21.
```
  403
   22
 +141
```

22.
```
  1,649
    118
 +  232
```

23.
```
  4,590
  1,682
 +    24
```

24.
```
  1,789
  2,538
 +4,666
```

25.
```
  10,569
 + 8,983
```

26.
```
  450,892
 +119,738
```

27.
```
  1,345,921
 +2,334,889
```

28. $41{,}237 + 12{,}999 + 8{,}001 =$

29. $3{,}289{,}873 + 444{,}555 + 319{,}009 =$

_____ _____

Problem Solving

Solve the following problems.

30. A special program was held at the Senior Center. Twenty-four people traveled to the program by car. Thirty-four took the bus. How many attended in all?

_____

31. Maria sold her car for $755. She sold her bike for $65. How much money did she get for the car and bike?

_____

32. Chris visited his family. His bus ticket cost $46. His meals were $26. What did the trip cost in all?

_____

33. Mrs. Patterson's Social Security check is $305 a month. Her husband gets $285 a month. How much do the two get from Social Security?

_____

The table below shows the number of circus tickets sold. Use the table to solve problems 34 and 35.

	Children	Adults
Friday	68,134	23,590
Saturday	76,168	45,097
Sunday	58,701	33,652

34. About how many tickets were sold on Saturday? Estimate to the nearest thousand.

_____

35. How many adults bought tickets during the three days? Give the exact answer and the estimate to the nearest thousand.

_____ _____

Subtraction

Find the difference.

1. $15 - 8 =$ _____

2. $9 - 7 =$ _____

3. $12 - 6 =$ _____

4. $7 - 0 =$ _____

5. $\begin{array}{r} 78 \\ -33 \\ \hline \end{array}$

6. $\begin{array}{r} 94 \\ -71 \\ \hline \end{array}$

7. $\begin{array}{r} 85 \\ -22 \\ \hline \end{array}$

8. $\begin{array}{r} 57 \\ -27 \\ \hline \end{array}$

9. $\begin{array}{r} 565 \\ -444 \\ \hline \end{array}$

10. $\begin{array}{r} 648 \\ -332 \\ \hline \end{array}$

11. $\begin{array}{r} 769 \\ -550 \\ \hline \end{array}$

12. $\begin{array}{r} 887 \\ -446 \\ \hline \end{array}$

13. $\begin{array}{r} 58 \\ -29 \\ \hline \end{array}$

14. $\begin{array}{r} 64 \\ -38 \\ \hline \end{array}$

15. $\begin{array}{r} 725 \\ -450 \\ \hline \end{array}$

16. $\begin{array}{r} 505 \\ -352 \\ \hline \end{array}$

17. $\begin{array}{r} 460 \\ -75 \\ \hline \end{array}$

18. $\begin{array}{r} 564 \\ -385 \\ \hline \end{array}$

19. $\begin{array}{r} 5,408 \\ -752 \\ \hline \end{array}$

20. $\begin{array}{r} 6,856 \\ -1,569 \\ \hline \end{array}$

21.	7,555 -2,666	22.	4,808 - 757	23.	8,621 -3,754	24.	6,930 -1,999

25.	38,404 -16,213	26.	88,005 -59,330	27.	80,763 -45,885

28.	54,321 -17,678	29.	545,890 -356,952	30.	694,386 -209,694

Problem Solving

Solve the following problems.

31. Maggie's Dress Shop is having a sale on dresses. A dress that was originally $86 is now $59. How much lower is the sale price?

32. Hank is saving for a new motorcycle. He has $545 saved. He needs $1,099. How much more does he need to save?

33. In the spring, the Brophy Tree farm had 2,500 trees. The owners cut down 895 trees. How many trees are left?

34. Mr. Riece wrote a check for $84. He had $350 in his account before he wrote this check. How much does he have in his account now?

35. Lu attended 15 classes last year. This year he attended 34 classes. How many more classes did he attend this year?

36. Paula bought her car five years ago. It had 18,000 miles on it. She just sold it with 72,000 miles. How many miles did she drive this car?

37. The last concert at the stadium was attended by 75,345 fans. This week's concert is expecting 94,975 fans. About how many more fans are expected at this concert? Estimate to the nearest thousand.

Renaming Before Subtracting

Before you can subtract, you must first rename. This means you "borrow" from one place value and give to another.

Examples

A. Rename 36 to show 10 more ones.

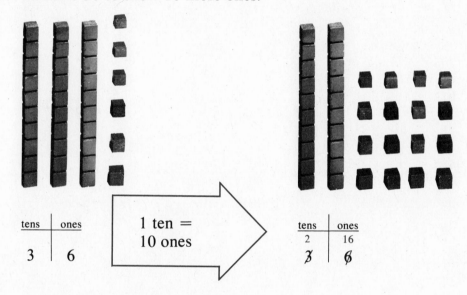

tens	ones
3	6

1 ten =
10 ones

tens	ones
2	16
3̶	6̶

B. Rename 315 to show 10 more tens.

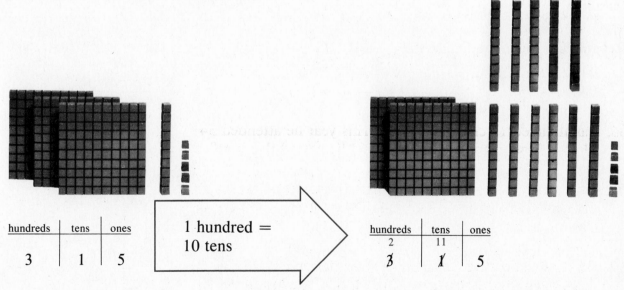

hundreds	tens	ones
3	1	5

1 hundred =
10 tens

hundreds	tens	ones
2	11	
3̶	1̶	5

C. Rename 3,265 to show ten more hundreds.

thousands	hundreds	tens	ones
3	2	6	5

1 thousand = 10 hundreds →

thousands	hundreds	tens	ones
2	12		
3̶	2̶	6	5

Rename to show more ones.

1. $\dfrac{1}{2̶}\ \dfrac{13}{3̶}$

2. $\underline{\quad}\ \underline{\quad}$
   9   5

3. $\underline{\quad}\ \underline{\quad}$
   5   0

4. $\underline{\quad}\ \underline{\quad}$
   4   4

5. $\underline{\quad}\ \underline{\quad}$
   8   2

6. $\underline{\quad}\ \underline{\quad}$
   7   1

7. $\underline{\quad}\ \underline{\quad}$
   2   8

8. $\underline{\quad}\ \underline{\quad}$
   3   7

Rename to show more tens.

9. $\dfrac{2}{3̶}\ \dfrac{16}{6̶}$ 5

10. $\underline{\quad}\ \underline{\quad}$
    5   7   9

11. $\underline{\quad}\ \underline{\quad}$
    9   3   5

12. $\underline{\quad}\ \underline{\quad}$
    8   8   6

13. $\underline{\quad}\ \underline{\quad}$
    4   5   8

14. $\underline{\quad}\ \underline{\quad}$
    6   0   5

15. $\underline{\quad}\ \underline{\quad}$
    8   1   2

16. $\underline{\quad}\ \underline{\quad}$
    9   2   4

Rename to show more hundreds.

17. $\dfrac{1}{2̶,}\ \dfrac{17}{7̶}$ 5   0

18. $\underline{\quad}\ \underline{\quad}$
    5,   4   0   3

19. $\underline{\quad}\ \underline{\quad}$
    8,   1   9   9

20. $\underline{\quad}\ \underline{\quad}$
    9,   0   8   7

21. $\underline{\quad}\ \underline{\quad}$
    6,   3   9   9

22. $\underline{\quad}\ \underline{\quad}$
    3,   5   9   1

23. $\underline{\quad}\ \underline{\quad}$
    7,   6   5   8

24. $\underline{\quad}\ \underline{\quad}$
    4,   2   7   0

25. $\underline{\quad}\ \underline{\quad}$
    7,   4   6   2

Subtraction With One Renaming

Sometimes we have to rename ones, tens, or hundreds to subtract.

Examples

A. 27 − 9 = ?

$$\begin{array}{r} {\scriptstyle 1\ 17} \\ 2\,7 \\ -\ \ 9 \\ \hline 1\,8 \end{array}$$ Rename to show more ones.
Then subtract.

B. 358 − 92 = ?

$$\begin{array}{r} {\scriptstyle 2\ 15} \\ 3\,5\,8 \\ -\ \ 9\,2 \\ \hline 2\,6\,6 \end{array}$$ Subtract the ones.
Rename to show more tens.
Then subtract.

C. 4,086 − 2,244 = ?

$$\begin{array}{r} {\scriptstyle 3\ \ 10} \\ 4\,,\,0\,8\,6 \\ -\ 2\,,\,2\,4\,4 \\ \hline 1\,,\,8\,4\,2 \end{array}$$ Subtract ones and tens.
Rename to show more hundreds.
Then subtract.

Practice

Subtract. Rename when necessary.

1.
$$\begin{array}{r} {\scriptstyle 2\ 18} \\ 3\,8 \\ -\ \ 9 \\ \hline 2\,9 \end{array}$$

2.
$$\begin{array}{r} 5\,2 \\ -\ \ 7 \\ \hline \end{array}$$

3.
$$\begin{array}{r} 6\,4 \\ -\ \ 6 \\ \hline \end{array}$$

4.
$$\begin{array}{r} 9\,7 \\ -\ \ 8 \\ \hline \end{array}$$

5.
$$\begin{array}{r} 7\,0 \\ -1\,5 \\ \hline \end{array}$$

6.
$$\begin{array}{r} 4\,6 \\ -2\,8 \\ \hline \end{array}$$

7.
$$\begin{array}{r} 9\,2 \\ -3\,5 \\ \hline \end{array}$$

8.
$$\begin{array}{r} 8\,4 \\ -5\,7 \\ \hline \end{array}$$

9.
$$\begin{array}{r} 3\,0\,6 \\ -\ \ 9\,4 \\ \hline \end{array}$$

10.
$$\begin{array}{r} 4\,2\,7 \\ -1\,8\,1 \\ \hline \end{array}$$

11.
$$\begin{array}{r} 2\,,\,3\,4\,7 \\ -\ \ \ 9\,1\,5 \\ \hline \end{array}$$

12.
$$\begin{array}{r} 9\,,\,5\,7\,8 \\ -2\,,\,7\,4\,4 \\ \hline \end{array}$$

Solve the following problems.

13. Tighe made $543 this week. He paid a car payment of $161. How much was left after the payment?

    _____

14. Guy paid $2,595 in taxes this year. Last year he paid $2,680. How much more did he pay last year?

    _____

15. Shawna owes the dentist $82 for her yearly checkup. She has paid $15. How much does she still owe?

    _____

16. Lucy does a weekly budget. She earns $267 a week. Her weekly expenses are $138. How much money does she have left at the end of the week?

    _____

17. Dave's yearly dues for a health club are $219. He has already paid $184. How much does he still owe?

    _____

18. Colleen had $697 in the bank. She purchased a new stereo system for $368. How much does she have left in the bank?

    _____

19. The Blendon Little League needs new uniforms. The total cost for uniforms is $3,687. The league has received $1,942 in contributions. How much more must be contributed?

    _____

20. Jamie's house needs a new furnace. It costs $5,053. He can get a bank loan for $3,250. How much does he still need in order to purchase the furnace?

    _____

LIFE SKILL

Figuring Postage

Postage is the charge for mailing a letter or package. Charges vary for different classes of mail. First-class postage costs more than third class. First-class mail goes faster.

The amount of postage depends on the weight. The table shows first-class and third-class postage for packages under 1 pound.

Parcel post rates for packages from one to two pounds are also given. These rates depend on the **zone,** or where the package is going. The higher the zone, the more the postage.

Use the tables to answer the questions.

1. Your package weighs 6 ounces. How much is first-class postage?

   _____

2. How much is third-class postage for a 6-ounce package?

   _____

3. How much can you save by mailing a 6-ounce package third class?

   _____

4. Your package weighs slightly more than a pound. It is going to zone 5. How much is parcel post?

   _____

5. How much can you save by mailing a 7-ounce package third class?

   _____

6. What does it cost to mail a one-pound package parcel post to zone 7?

   _____

Oz.	First Class	Third Class
1	.29	
2	.52	
3	.75	
4	.98	
5	1.21	1.15
6	1.44	1.15
7	1.67	1.25
8	1.90	1.25
9	2.13	1.42
10	2.36	1.42
11	2.59	1.62
12	2.90	1.62
13	2.90	1.90
14	2.90	1.90
15	2.90	2.25
16	2.90	2.25

Parcel Post	(1-2 pounds)
Local	1.90
Zones 1 & 2	2.20
Zone 3	2.45
Zone 4	2.65
Zone 5	2.90
Zone 6	3.15
Zone 7	3.15
Zone 8	3.15

Subtraction With More Than One Renaming

When you have to rename more than once, follow these steps:

Step 1 Rename to show more ones. Then, subtract the ones.

Step 2 Rename to show more tens. Then subtract the tens.

Step 3 Subtract the hundreds.

--- **Example** ---

Subtract. $643 - 479 = ?$

Step 1
$13 - 9 = 4$

$$
\begin{array}{r}
6\,\overset{3}{\cancel{4}}\,\overset{13}{\cancel{3}} \\
-\,4\,7\,9 \\
\hline
4
\end{array}
$$

Step 2
$13 - 7 = 6$

$$
\begin{array}{r}
\overset{13}{} \\
5\,\overset{3}{\cancel{4}}\,\overset{13}{\cancel{3}} \\
\cancel{6}\,\cancel{4}\,\cancel{3} \\
-\,4\,7\,9 \\
\hline
6\,4
\end{array}
$$

Step 3
$5 - 4 = 1$

$$
\begin{array}{r}
\overset{13}{} \\
5\,\overset{3}{\cancel{4}}\,\overset{13}{\cancel{3}} \\
\cancel{6}\,\cancel{4}\,\cancel{3} \\
-\,4\,7\,9 \\
\hline
1\,6\,4
\end{array}
$$

--- **Practice** ---

Subtract.

1. 547 −179	**2.** 835 −357	**3.** 444 −177	**4.** 673 −398
5. 531 −288	**6.** 346 −259	**7.** 814 −246	**8.** 572 −195
9. 7,256 −3,847	**10.** 6,442 −3,099	**11.** 9,191 −3,262	**12.** 2,468 −1,785

13.	7,622 −1,888	14.	5,945 − 268	15.	8,359 −4,890	16.	4,151 −2,222

Problem Solving

Solve the following problems.

17. Michael was comparing prices to have a deck installed. Company A bid $2,679, and Company B bid $3,120. How much would he save by having Company A build his deck?

_____

18. Last month Gail spent $355 on traveling expenses. This month she spent $298. How much more did she spend last month?

_____

19. Greg deposited $198 into his checking account. His balance is now $443. What was his balance before deposit?

_____

20. The state of Delaware is approximately 2,844 square miles. The state of Rhode Island is about 1,545 square miles. What is the difference in size?

_____

21. North Carolina became a state in 1789. How many years was it a state in 1965?

_____

22. Julio bought a car for $5,642. He purchased another car for $9,721. What was the difference in price?

_____

Subtraction: Renaming With Zeros

When you subtract from zero, borrow from the next place value.

─────────── **Example** ───────────

Subtract. 5,002 − 4,649 = ?

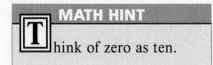

Step 1
Rename to show
more hundreds.

$$\overset{4}{\cancel{5}},\overset{10}{\cancel{0}}02$$
$$-4,649$$

Step 2
Rename to show
more tens.

$$\overset{4}{\cancel{5}},\overset{\overset{9}{\cancel{10}}}{\cancel{0}}\overset{10}{\cancel{0}}2$$
$$-4,649$$

Step 3
Rename to show
more ones.

$$\overset{4}{\cancel{5}},\overset{\overset{9}{\cancel{10}}}{\cancel{0}}\overset{\overset{9}{\cancel{10}}}{\cancel{0}}\overset{12}{2}$$
$$-4,649$$

Step 4
Subtract.

$$\overset{4}{\cancel{5}},\overset{\overset{9}{\cancel{10}}}{\cancel{0}}\overset{\overset{9}{\cancel{10}}}{\cancel{0}}\overset{12}{\cancel{2}}$$
$$-4,649$$
$$\overline{353}$$

─────────── **Practice** ───────────

Subtract.

1. 805
   −116

2. 600
   −467

3. 8,003
   −5,680

4. 3,002
   −1,556

5. 9,090 − 643 = _____

6. 605 − 390 = _____

7. 6,004 − 789 = _____

─────────── **Problem Solving** ───────────

Solve the following problems.

8. The State Park has 500 campsites. On
   Labor Day weekend all but 12 are
   taken. How many are taken?

9. Teri was born in 1980. Her mother was
   born in 1947. How many years older is
   Teri's mother than Teri?

_____

_____

Checking Subtraction

Subtraction can be checked by adding.

Examples

A. Subtract.   Add.

```
   3 6 5          2 9 1
 - 2 9 1        +   7 4
 ─────────      ─────────
     7 4          3 6 5
```

B. Subtract.   Add.

```
   1 , 3 2 5          1 , 0 7 5
 -     2 5 0        +     2 5 0
 ─────────────      ─────────────
   1 , 0 7 5          1 , 3 2 5
```

Practice

Check each answer by adding. If it is correct, put √ in the blank. If it is not correct, find the answer and put it in the blank.

1.
```
   2 2 0              4 5
 -   4 5          + 1 7 5
 ─────────        ─────────
   1 7 5  √         2 2 0
```

2.
```
   4 , 1 5 0
 -     9 7 5
 ───────────
   3 , 1 7 4 _____
```

3.
```
   3 3 2
 -   2 9
 ─────────
   3 1 3  _____
```

4.
```
   6 5 1
 - 2 1 3
 ─────────
   4 3 8  _____
```

5.
```
   5 , 9 0 4
 - 1 , 8 5 5
 ───────────
   4 , 1 4 9 _____
```

6.
```
   9 , 0 0 1
 -     5 6 7
 ───────────
   8 , 4 3 4 _____
```

7.
```
   7 , 1 3 4
 -     7 6 8
 ───────────
   7 , 4 6 6 _____
```

8.
```
   6 , 4 6 6
 - 3 , 7 8 8
 ───────────
   2 , 6 7 8 _____
```

9.
```
   4 0 0
 - 1 6 4
 ─────────
   2 3 6  _____
```

10.
```
   8 8 8
 - 6 9 7
 ─────────
   1 9 1  _____
```

11.
```
   1 , 0 9 5
 -     8 7 3
 ───────────
       2 1 3 _____
```

12.
```
   7 0 6
 - 2 7 7
 ─────────
   4 2 9  _____
```

Subtracting Large Numbers

Subtract large numbers the same way you subtract small numbers.
Use your renaming skills the same way. There are more digits to
work with. Line up the digits by place value and then subtract from
right to left.

Examples

A. Subtract.
$$\begin{array}{r} 9\,8,8\overset{7\;\;17\;14\;15}{\cancel{8}\cancel{5}\cancel{5}} \\ -\,5\,7,9\,8\,6 \\ \hline 4\,0,8\,6\,9 \end{array}$$

MATH HINT

Subtract the ones,
borrow if necessary.
Subtract the tens, borrow
if necessary.
Subtract the hundreds,
borrow if necessary, and
so on.

B. 824,093 people filled out cards for the
Heart Association. Of these, 271,124
were smokers. How many were not
smokers?

$$\begin{array}{r} 8\overset{7\;12\;3\;\;\;10\;8\;13}{2\,4,0\,9\,3} \\ -\,2\,7\,1,1\,2\,4 \\ \hline 5\,5\,2,9\,6\,9 \end{array} \text{ nonsmokers}$$

Practice

Subtract.

1. $\begin{array}{r} 6,325,690 \\ -1,674,369 \\ \hline \end{array}$

2. $\begin{array}{r} 45,789,314 \\ -\ 5,895,321 \\ \hline \end{array}$

3. $\begin{array}{r} 95,467,333 \\ -89,684,102 \\ \hline \end{array}$

4. $\begin{array}{r} 62,854 \\ -12,740 \\ \hline \end{array}$

5. $\begin{array}{r} 10,888 \\ -\ 9,975 \\ \hline \end{array}$

6. $\begin{array}{r} 97,853 \\ -\ 9,174 \\ \hline \end{array}$

7. 75,600 − 64,950 = _____   **8.** 799,367 − 366,988 = _____

9. $\begin{array}{r} 102,458,912 \\ -\ 30,245,610 \\ \hline \end{array}$ **10.** $\begin{array}{r} 5,783,502 \\ -1,679,472 \\ \hline \end{array}$ **11.** $\begin{array}{r} 754,873 \\ -469,378 \\ \hline \end{array}$

12. $\begin{array}{r} 80,544,422 \\ -56,777,113 \\ \hline \end{array}$ **13.** $\begin{array}{r} 403,555,678 \\ -\ 97,444,589 \\ \hline \end{array}$

Problem Solving

Solve the following problems.

14. Toni had 59,870 miles on his truck before his trip. He had 60,421 miles on the truck when he came back. How far did he drive? _____

15. In a community election, Patricelli received 58,967,489 votes. Schulz received 60,488,099 votes. By how many votes did Schulz win? _____

16. At one time, the population of Finland was 4,977,325. Almost 489,965 people lived in its major city of Helsinki. How many people lived in the rest of the country? _____

17. In a geography class, Joe was asked the difference in land area between Brazil and Peru. Brazil's total land area is 3,286,488 square miles. Peru's land area is 496,225 square miles. Help Joe determine the difference. _____

18. During one year, the Houston airport handled 16,007,355 passengers. The Phoenix airport handled 20,710,790 passengers. How many more passengers used the Phoenix airport? _____

LESSON 29

Estimating in Subtraction

As in addition, you can estimate to check the answers in subtraction problems. You can estimate in subtraction by following these steps:

Step 1 Round the numbers you are working with to the nearest place value. You might be asked to round to the nearest ten, hundred, thousand, or so forth.

Step 2 Look to the right of the place value of the number you are working with.
If the number is 5 or more, round up.
If the number is less than 5, round down.

Step 3 Subtract your rounded answers to get the estimated answer.

 **MATH HINT**

An estimated answer can be checked by finding the exact answer.

─────────────── **Examples** ───────────────

A. Estimate by rounding to the nearest hundred.
$$5,359$$
$$-2,849$$

Step 1 Find the hundreds place, because this is where you were asked to round.

$$5,\overset{\downarrow}{3}59$$
$$-2,849$$

Step 2 Look to the right of this place value.
If the number is 5 or more, round up.
If the number is less than 5, round down.

$5,359$ 5 is equal to 5, so round up—5,400
$-2,849$ 4 is less than 5, so round down—2,800

88

Step 3   Subtract the rounded answers to get the estimated answer.

Estimate	Exact
5,400	5,359
−2,800	−2,849
2,600	2,510 is close to our estimate of 2,600

B. Calley makes $232 a week. She spends $168 a week. How much is left over? (Round the numbers to the nearest ten.)

Estimate	Exact
230	232
−170	−168
60	64

Practice

Estimate the answers by rounding to the nearest ten. Then find the exact answers.

1.
```
 5 4 8      5 5 0
-1 2 9     -1 3 0
 4 1 9      4 2 0
```

2.
```
 9 6 5
-1 7 5
```

3.
```
 8 6 6
-5 4 9
```

Estimate the answers by rounding to the nearest hundred. Then find the exact answers.

4.
```
 9 8 7
-3 4 8
```

5.
```
 9,7 8 5
-   5 0 9
```

6.
```
 3,5 0 8
-1,6 9 8
```

Estimate the answers by rounding to the nearest thousand. Then find the exact answers.

7.
```
 2 0,9 8 6
-  3,2 5 1
```

8.
```
 5 2,9 8 2
-1 5,2 2 0
```

9.
```
 1 0 9,3 0 8
-  9 6,7 9 5
```

Solve the following problems using estimation.

10. Rami spent $176 to fly to Las Vegas. She spent $99 for the bus back. What is the difference in cost of the bus fare and the air fare? To the nearest ten, estimate the difference.

_____

11. The members of the Sports Booster Club sponsored a car wash. They washed 219 cars, 123 trucks, and 15 vans. To the nearest ten, estimate the total number of vehicles washed.

_____

12. Five years ago, Nathan began a stamp collection. Year 1, he collected 165 stamps; Year 2, 330 stamps; Year 3, 280 stamps; Year 4, 125 stamps; and Year 5, 290 stamps. To the nearest hundred, estimate the total amount of stamps collected.

_____

Problem Solving—Choosing the Operation

Review the steps for problem solving. Notice that Step 2 asks you to make a plan to solve the problem. You are actually choosing the operation that will give you the problem's solution.

Step 1 Read the problem and underline the key words. These words will usually relate to some mathematics reasoning computation.

Step 2 Make a plan to solve the problem. Ask yourself, Should I add, subtract, multiply, divide, round, or compare? You may have to do more than one of these operations for the same problem.

Step 3 Find the solution. Use your math knowledge to find your answer.

Step 4 Check the answer. Ask yourself, Is the answer reasonable? Did you find what you were asked for?

Example

The table below shows how much four workers earned in one year. It also shows how much they paid in taxes. Using the table, determine how much more Soto earned than Lopez.

Worker	Pay	Federal tax	State tax
Wong	$12,000	$1,372	$120
Johnson	$11,000	$1,080	$110
Soto	$13,000	$1,448	$130
Lopéz	$12,500	$1,402	$125

Step 1 Determine how much more Soto earns than Lopez. The key words are **more than.**

Step 2 Remember this step is asking you to choose the operation to perform. The key words indicate which operation should occur—subtraction.

Step 3 Find the solution.

$$
\begin{array}{r}
\$13,000 \\
-\ 12,500 \\
\hline
\$\quad\ 500
\end{array}
$$

Soto earned $500 more than Lopez.

Step 4 Check the answer. You can check subtraction with addition.

$$
\begin{array}{r}
\$12,500 \\
+\quad\ 500 \\
\hline
\$13,000
\end{array}
$$

--- **Practice** ---

Using the table, answer the following problems.

1. How much more federal tax does Soto pay than Lopéz? _____

2. How much do all four workers make before taxes? Estimate to the nearest thousand dollars. _____

3. How much state tax do the workers pay in all? _____

4. How much federal tax do the workers pay in all? Estimate to the nearest hundred dollars. _____

5. How much more federal tax does Lopéz pay than Johnson? _____

Posttest

Find the difference.

1. $16 - 9 =$ _____ **2.** $11 - 6 =$ _____ **3.** $14 - 8 =$ _____ **4.** $9 - 0 =$ _____

5. $\begin{array}{r} 8\,7 \\ -\,4\,4 \\ \hline \end{array}$

6. $\begin{array}{r} 4\,9 \\ -\,1\,7 \\ \hline \end{array}$

7. $\begin{array}{r} 5\,8 \\ -\,3\,3 \\ \hline \end{array}$

8. $\begin{array}{r} 7\,5 \\ -\,6\,5 \\ \hline \end{array}$

9. $\begin{array}{r} 6\,7\,5 \\ -\,4\,4\,4 \\ \hline \end{array}$

10. $\begin{array}{r} 8\,4\,7 \\ -\,2\,3\,6 \\ \hline \end{array}$

11. $\begin{array}{r} 5\,7\,9 \\ -\,2\,6\,0 \\ \hline \end{array}$

12. $\begin{array}{r} 6\,6\,4 \\ -\,5\,5\,3 \\ \hline \end{array}$

13. $\begin{array}{r} 5\,5 \\ -\,1\,9 \\ \hline \end{array}$

14. $\begin{array}{r} 7\,3 \\ -\,4\,7 \\ \hline \end{array}$

15. $\begin{array}{r} 5\,6\,8 \\ -\,2\,3\,9 \\ \hline \end{array}$

16. $\begin{array}{r} 4\,0\,7 \\ -\,3\,5\,2 \\ \hline \end{array}$

17. $\begin{array}{r} 6\,4\,0 \\ -\ \ 8\,8 \\ \hline \end{array}$

18. $\begin{array}{r} 7\,2\,4 \\ -\,6\,5\,5 \\ \hline \end{array}$

19. $\begin{array}{r} 6,3\,0\,9 \\ -\ \ \ \,8\,2\,1 \\ \hline \end{array}$

20. $\begin{array}{r} 5,7\,3\,4 \\ -\,1,2\,5\,5 \\ \hline \end{array}$

21. $\begin{array}{r} 8,5\,7\,4 \\ -\,2,8\,9\,6 \\ \hline \end{array}$

22. $\begin{array}{r} 6,4\,0\,7 \\ -\ \ \ \,8\,5\,8 \\ \hline \end{array}$

23. $\begin{array}{r} 9,4\,3\,1 \\ -\,6,7\,4\,5 \\ \hline \end{array}$

24. $\begin{array}{r} 5,8\,1\,0 \\ -\,3,9\,9\,9 \\ \hline \end{array}$

25. $\begin{array}{r} 4\,8,5\,0\,5 \\ -\,2\,6,4\,1\,3 \\ \hline \end{array}$

26. $\begin{array}{r} 6\,6,0\,0\,2 \\ -\,4\,8,5\,5\,0 \\ \hline \end{array}$

27. $\begin{array}{r} 9\,0,6\,5\,2 \\ -\,3\,5,7\,8\,5 \\ \hline \end{array}$

28.   43,671
        −22,985
---
29.   435,670
        −240,859
---
30.   763,555
        −288,458

31. 1,855,462 − 899,020 = _____   **32.** 53,678,092 − 24,055,854 = _____

Problem Solving

Solve the following problems.

33. A $349 microwave oven was marked down to $279. How much lower was the sale price?   _____

34. Carolyn had $29 before she went shopping. She had $15 left after shopping. How much did she spend?   _____

35. Murray had $585 in the bank. He took out $140. How much was left?   _____

36. Omar's rent was $290 a month. It went up to $325. How much more a month does Omar have to pay?   _____

37. Mr. Krumbien owns a chicken farm. He had 109 dozen eggs for sale last week. He sold 83 dozen. How many dozens were left?   _____

38. A bowl found in 1963 was made in A.D. 445. Estimate the age of the bowl to the nearest ten years.   _____

39. Leo bought his house for $37,590. He sold it thirty years later for $112,969. About how much profit did he make? Estimate to the nearest thousand.   _____

Addition and Subtraction Posttest

Write the numbers or words.

1. forty-five _____

2. one hundred sixty-five _____

3. 58 _____

4. 8,652 _____

Fill in the blanks with > or <.

5. 31 _____ 13

6. 1,099 _____ 1,999

What number is in the tens place? What number is in the thousands place?

7. 5,819

_____   _____
tens   thousands

8. 364,892

_____   _____
tens   thousands

Round these numbers to the nearest million and ten thousand.

9. 49,804,644

_____   _____
million   ten thousand

10. 302,164,899

_____   _____
million   ten thousand

Add or subtract.

11. $\begin{array}{r} 1\,3 \\ +\,2\,1 \\ \hline \end{array}$

12. $\begin{array}{r} 8\,0 \\ +\,3\,0 \\ \hline \end{array}$

13. $\begin{array}{r} 6\,9 \\ -\,3\,3 \\ \hline \end{array}$

14. $\begin{array}{r} 9\,0 \\ -\,4\,0 \\ \hline \end{array}$

15. $\begin{array}{r} 6\,8 \\ -\,2\,6 \\ \hline \end{array}$

16. $\begin{array}{r} 7\,4\,5 \\ +\,\;\,2\,3 \\ \hline \end{array}$

17. $\begin{array}{r} 6\,6\,8 \\ -\,4\,5\,1 \\ \hline \end{array}$

18. $\begin{array}{r} 8\,4\,3 \\ +\,\;\,5\,8 \\ \hline \end{array}$

19. 340 + 65 = _____

20. 655 − 321 = _____

Add or subtract. Check your work.

21. $$\begin{array}{r} 7\,8 \\ -\,2\,5 \\ \hline \end{array}$$

22. $$\begin{array}{r} 2\,5 \\ 4\,1 \\ +\,5\,2 \\ \hline \end{array}$$

23. $$\begin{array}{r} 4\,0\,8 \\ -\,2\,8\,3 \\ \hline \end{array}$$

24. $$\begin{array}{r} 7\,0\,8 \\ 1\,1\,3 \\ +\,1\,6\,5 \\ \hline \end{array}$$

25. $$\begin{array}{r} 4{,}0\,0\,1 \\ -\,1{,}0\,1\,4 \\ \hline \end{array}$$

26. $$\begin{array}{r} 1\,0\,8{,}5\,4\,4 \\ -\;\;1\,3{,}6\,1\,3 \\ \hline \end{array}$$

27. $$\begin{array}{r} 4{,}9\,1\,6 \\ 3\,1\,7 \\ +\,2{,}6\,5\,9 \\ \hline \end{array}$$

28. $$\begin{array}{r} 7\,8\,7{,}2\,9\,0 \\ 3\,8{,}4\,4\,5 \\ +\,3\,5\,8{,}9\,0\,1 \\ \hline \end{array}$$

29. $846 + 32 + 85 + 9{,}134 =$ _____

30. $56{,}948{,}320 - 18{,}647{,}525 =$ _____

Write four different number sentences using 15, 5, 10.

31. _____   _____   _____   _____

Problem Solving

The table below shows the number of amusement park tickets sold.
Use the table to solve problems 32–35.

	Adults	Children
June	22,665	69,444
July	42,050	77,265
August	36,245	57,901

32. About how many tickets were sold in all? Estimate to the nearest thousand.

33. How many more children than adults were at the amusement park in June?

_____   _____

34. How many adults bought tickets during the 3 months?

35. How many tickets were sold in August?

_____   _____

Multiplication and Division Basic Facts

Multiply.

1. $1 \times 5 =$ _____

2. $9 \times 6 =$ _____

3. $8 \times 5 =$ _____

4. $2 \times 6 =$ _____

5. $7 \times 3 =$ _____

6. $5 \times 4 =$ _____

7. $4 \times 9 =$ _____

8. $3 \times 3 =$ _____

9. $\begin{array}{r} 7 \\ \times 7 \\ \hline \end{array}$

10. $\begin{array}{r} 9 \\ \times 8 \\ \hline \end{array}$

11. $\begin{array}{r} 4 \\ \times 0 \\ \hline \end{array}$

12. $\begin{array}{r} 5 \\ \times 5 \\ \hline \end{array}$

Divide.

13. $15 \div 3 =$ _____

14. $24 \div 8 =$ _____

15. $36 \div 4 =$ _____

16. $42 \div 6 =$ _____

17. $64 \div 8 =$ _____

18. $81 \div 9 =$ _____

19. $20 \div 5 =$ _____

20. $30 \div 6 =$ _____

21. $0 \div 6 =$ _____

22. $54 \div 9 =$ _____

23. $72 \div 8 =$ _____

24. $6 \div 6 =$ _____

Write four different number sentences using 6, 8, 48.

25. _____   _____   _____   _____

Complete these number sentences.

26. $3 \times 4 = $ _____   **27.** $63 \div 7 = $ _____   **28.** $56 \div 8 = $ _____   **29.** $49 \div 7 = $ _____

30. _____ $\times 4 = 24$ **31.** _____ $\times 6 = 6$ **32.** _____ $\times 7 = 21$ **33.** _____ $\div 5 = 8$

34. $35 \div$ _____ $= 7$ **35.** $72 \div$ _____ $= 8$ **36.** $4 \div$ _____ $= 4$ **37.** $6 \times$ _____ $= 18$

Problem Solving

Solve the following problems.

38. Eduardo gives Spanish lessons. He charges $7 a lesson for each student. There are 9 students in his class. How much does he earn for each class?

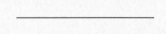

39. Helen charges $3 per page for word processing. She earned $27. How many pages did she process?

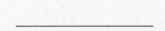

40. Dimitri earned $64 for 8 hours of work. What does he make per hour?

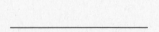

41. A dinner costs $96 for 8 people. What was the cost per person?   _____

Basic Multiplication Skills

Think of multiplication as repeated addition. When you multiply, you are actually taking a shortcut to addition.

Example

Dick bought 4 packs of juice. Each pack had 6 cans. How many cans did he buy in all?

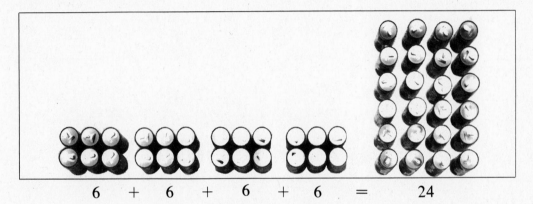

$4 \times 6 = 24$
$6 \times 4 = 24$

$$\begin{array}{r} 4 \\ \times 6 \\ \hline 24 \end{array} \qquad \begin{array}{r} 6 \\ \times 4 \\ \hline 24 \end{array}$$

$$6 \quad + \quad 6 \quad + \quad 6 \quad + \quad 6 \quad = \quad 24$$

You can find the answer by adding. Add the number 6 four times.
$6 + 6 + 6 + 6 = 24$

But there is a shorter way. We can **multiply 6 times 4.** $6 \times 4 = 24$. We read this number sentence "6 times 4 equals 24."

Multiplication is a short way to add. It doesn't matter what order the numbers are in. Both $6 \times 4 = 24$ and $4 \times 6 = 24$.

There are two more things to know about multiplication.
  Any number times zero equals zero. So $5 \times 0 = 0$ and $0 \times 7 = 0$.
  Any number times one equals the number. So $6 \times 1 = 6$.

Fill in the blanks in each set of problems. Compare the answers.

1. $3 + 3 =$ _____
   $3 \times 2 =$ _____
   $2 \times$ _____ $= 6$

2. $5 + 5 =$ _____
   $5 \times 2 =$ _____
   $2 \times$ _____ $= 10$

3. $7 + 7 =$ _____
   $7 \times 2 =$ _____
   $2 \times$ _____ $= 14$

4. $4 + 4 =$ _____
   $4 \times 2 =$ _____
   $2 \times$ _____ $= 8$

5. $6 + 6 =$ _____
   $6 \times 2 =$ _____
   $2 \times$ _____ $= 12$

6. $8 + 8 =$ _____
   $8 \times 2 =$ _____
   $2 \times$ _____ $= 16$

Find the answers and compare them.

7. $3 + 3 + 3 =$ _____
   $3 \times 3 =$ _____

8. $6 + 6 + 6 =$ _____
   $6 \times 3 =$ _____

9. $9 + 9 + 9 =$ _____
   $9 \times 3 =$ _____

10. $4 + 4 + 4 =$ _____
    $4 \times 3 =$ _____

11. $7 + 7 + 7 =$ _____
    $7 \times 3 =$ _____

12. $1 + 1 + 1 =$ _____
    $1 \times 3 =$ _____

13. $5 + 5 + 5 =$ _____
    $5 \times 3 =$ _____

14. $8 + 8 + 8 =$ _____
    $8 \times 3 =$ _____

15. $0 + 0 + 0 =$ _____
    $0 \times 3 =$ _____

Complete these multiplication facts.

16. $5 \times 5 =$ _____

17. $7 \times 2 =$ _____

18. $7 \times 1 =$ _____

19. $5 \times 6 =$ _____

20. $7 \times 3 =$ _____

21. $8 \times 6 =$ _____

22. $5 \times 7 =$ _____

23. $7 \times 4 =$ _____

24. $8 \times 8 =$ _____

25. $5 \times 8 =$ _____

26. $7 \times 5 =$ _____

27. $8 \times 9 =$ _____

28. $5 \times 9 =$ _____

29. $7 \times 6 =$ _____

30. $9 \times 1 =$ _____

31. $6 \times 0 =$ _____

32. $7 \times 7 =$ _____

33. $9 \times 2 =$ _____

34. $6 \times 7 =$ _____

35. $7 \times 8 =$ _____

36. $9 \times 3 =$ _____

37. $6 \times 8 =$ _____

38. $7 \times 9 =$ _____

39. $9 \times 4 =$ _____

40. $6 \times 9 =$ _____

41. $8 \times 0 =$ _____

42. $9 \times 5 =$ _____

43. $8 \times 4 =$ _____

44. $8 \times 5 =$ _____

45. $9 \times 6 =$ _____

Solve the following problems. Write your multiplication equation.

46. Mr. Lejeune runs a dry cleaning shop. He charges $4 for each suit. One morning he took in 7 suits. How much did he make?

   $7 \times \$4 = \$28$

47. Julia takes the bus to work. It costs $2 one-way each day. What does it cost her to get to work Monday through Friday?

   _____

48. Mr. Mason earns $6 an hour. Thursday he worked 8 hours. How much did he earn on Thursday?

   _____

49. Myra spends $3 a day on lunch. How much does she spend on lunch Monday through Friday?

   _____

50. Alphonse wants to lose 4 pounds a week. His diet program lasts 3 weeks. How much does Alphonse hope to lose?

   _____

Basic Division Skills

Think of division as repeated subtraction.

---- **Example** ----

A family ate 15 pancakes for breakfast. Each person ate 3 pancakes. How many people are in the family?

You can find the answer by subtracting 3 pancakes at a time. Subtract until there are none left.

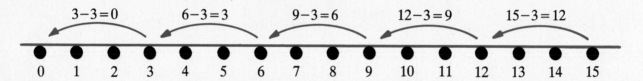

$$3-3=0 \qquad 6-3=3 \qquad 9-3=6 \qquad 12-3=9 \qquad 15-3=12$$

0 1 2 3 4 5 6 7 8 9 10 11 12 13 14 15

You subtract 3 from 15 five times. There are five 3's in 15.

There is a shorter way to find the answer. You can divide 15 by 3.
Division is a short way to subtract.

How many 3's
in 15?
$15 \div 3 = 5$
15 divided by
3 = 5
5 threes in 15

How many 1's
in 15?
$15 \div 1 = 15$
15 ones in 15

How many 15's
in 15?
$15 \div 15 = 1$
1 fifteen in 15

How many 15's
in 0?
$0 \div 15 = 0$
0 fifteens in 0

How many 2's are

1. in 6?
   6 ÷ 2 = _____

2. in 8?
   8 ÷ 2 = _____

3. in 10?
   10 ÷ 2 = _____

4. in 12?
   12 ÷ 2 = _____

5. in 14?
   14 ÷ 2 = _____

6. in 16?
   16 ÷ 2 = _____

Divide.

7. 6 ÷ 3 = _____

8. 8 ÷ 4 = _____

9. 10 ÷ 5 = _____

10. 9 ÷ 3 = _____

11. 12 ÷ 4 = _____

12. 15 ÷ 5 = _____

13. 12 ÷ 3 = _____

14. 16 ÷ 4 = _____

15. 20 ÷ 5 = _____

16. 15 ÷ 3 = _____

17. 20 ÷ 4 = _____

18. 25 ÷ 5 = _____

19. 18 ÷ 3 = _____

20. 24 ÷ 4 = _____

21. 30 ÷ 5 = _____

22. 21 ÷ 3 = _____

23. 28 ÷ 4 = _____

24. 35 ÷ 5 = _____

25. 24 ÷ 3 = _____

26. 32 ÷ 4 = _____

27. 40 ÷ 5 = _____

28. 27 ÷ 3 = _____

29. 36 ÷ 4 = _____

30. 45 ÷ 5 = _____

Problem Solving

Solve the following problems. Write your division equation.

31. Irella spends $36 a month on movies. There are 4 weeks in a
    month. How much does she spend per week? $36 ÷ 4 = $9

32. A sign reads, "3 for $24." How much for one?   _____

33. Cindy did some laundry. Each machine she used cost $2. She
    spent $18. How many machines did she use?   _____

LIFE SKILL

Using Drugs Safely

Every drug sold has a label that tells how much of the drug to take at one time. It tells how to use the drug safely.

Read the label. Answer questions 1–3.

> **Directions:** For relief of minor
>   headache, neuralgia
> Adults: 2 tablets every 3 hours.
> Children, 10 to 16 years: 1 tablet.
> Children, 6 to 10 years: $\frac{1}{2}$ tablet.
> Children's doses no more than 3
>   times a day.

1. How many tablets can an adult take safely in 24 hours?

2. How many tablets should an adult take at one time?

3. Should a 14-year old take these tablets more than 4 times a day?

Read the label. Answer questions 4–6.

> **Dosage:**
> Adults: 2 tablets every 4 hours. No
>   more than 8 tablets in 24 hours.
> Children 6 to 12 years: 1 tablet.
>   Do not give to children under 6.
>   No more than 4 tablets every 24
>   hours.

4. Mr. Hunt took 2 tablets at noon. When can he take the next dose?

5. How many hours apart should children's doses be spaced in 24 hours?

6. How many tablets can a 5 year-old take in 24 hours?

Read the label. Answer questions 7–10.

> **Directions:**
> Adults, 12 years and over:
> Dosage 2 teaspoons. No more than 16 teaspoons a day.
> Children, 6 to 12 years:
> Dosage 1 teaspoon. No more than 6 teaspoons a day.

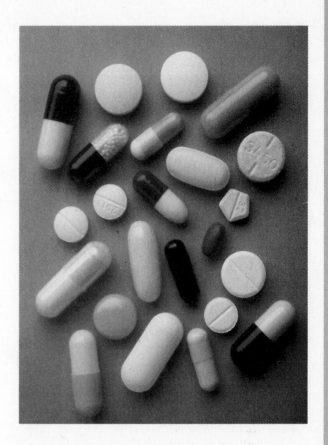

7. How many dosages in 24 hours can an adult safely take this medicine?

8. What is the normal dosage for an adult?

9. What is the child's dosage for this medicine?

10. Should a 4-year-old take this medicine?

11. Should a 10-year-old use this spray?

12. How many hours apart should an adult's doses be spaced?

13. Can an adult use this spray for a week?

14. The doctor prescribed the spray to be taken 4 times a day. How many hours apart is this?

Read the label. Answer questions 11–14.

> **Adults:**
> Spray every 8 hours or as told by a doctor. Keep head and bottle up. Spray each nostril quickly, sniff upward.
> **Warning:** For Adult use only. Do not give to children under 12. Do not use this product for more than three days.

Multiplication and Division

These are **number sentences** for multiplication and division.

$$24 \div 3 = 8 \qquad 9 \times 4 = 36$$

The three numbers in one number sentence can be used to write three more sentences. They make a **family of facts.**

Examples

A. $24 \div 3 = 8$
   $24 \div 8 = 3$
   $8 \times 3 = 24$
   $3 \times 8 = 24$

B. $9 \times 4 = 36$
   $4 \times 9 = 36$
   $36 \div 9 = 4$
   $36 \div 4 = 9$

Practice

Complete each family of facts.

1. $8 \times 2 = $ _____

   $2 \times 8 = $ _____

   $16 \div 2 = $ _____

   $16 \div 8 = $ _____

2. $4 \times 3 = $ _____

   $3 \times 4 = $ _____

   $12 \div 4 = $ _____

   $12 \div 3 = $ _____

3. $6 \times 3 = $ _____

   $3 \times 6 = $ _____

   $18 \div 6 = $ _____

   $18 \div 3 = $ _____

4. $27 \div 3 = $ _____

   $27 \div 9 = $ _____

   $3 \times 9 = $ _____

   $9 \times 3 = $ _____

5. $54 \div 9 = $ _____

   $54 \div 6 = $ _____

   $6 \times 9 = $ _____

   $9 \times 6 = $ _____

6. $6 \times $ _____ $= 48$

   $48 \div $ _____ $= 6$

   $8 \times $ _____ $= 48$

   $48 \div 8 = $ _____

7. _____ × 8 = 72

_____ ÷ 9 = 8

72 ÷ 8 = _____

_____ × 9 = 72

8. 7 × _____ = 14

14 ÷ 7 = _____

14 ÷ 2 = _____

2 × _____ = 14

9. _____ × 5 = 20

_____ ÷ 5 = 4

_____ × 4 = 20

_____ ÷ 4 = 5

Multiply or divide.

10. 2 × 1 = _____

11. _____ × 4 = 0

12. 8 × _____ = 0

13. 4 ÷ 2 = _____

14. _____ ÷ 4 = 9

15. 42 ÷ _____ = 6

16. 8 ÷ 2 = _____

17. _____ × 4 = 28

18. 8 × _____ = 48

19. 18 ÷ 2 = _____

20. _____ × 4 = 16

21. 54 ÷ _____ = 9

22. 10 ÷ 2 = _____

23. _____ × 5 = 5

24. 9 × _____ = 81

25. 3 × 2 = _____

26. _____ ÷ 5 = 3

27. 63 ÷ _____ = 7

28. 9 × 3 = _____

29. _____ ÷ 5 = 6

30. 8 × _____ = 64

Write four different number sentences using the following numbers.

31. 7, 8, 56

_____ 7 × 8 = 56 _____

_____ 8 × 7 = 56 _____

_____ 56 ÷ 7 = 8 _____

_____ 56 ÷ 8 = 7 _____

32. 4, 9, 36

_____

_____

_____

_____

33. 5, 40, 8

_____

_____

_____

_____

34. 42, 6, 7

_____

_____

_____

35. 9, 3, 27

_____

_____

_____

36. 5, 30, 6

_____

_____

_____

Number Series

Many tests for job and school will ask you to find the next number in a series. To find the number, look for a pattern to the numbers in a series.

Look at the first two numbers. See how they relate. Then look at the second two numbers. See how they relate. Find the pattern between the two sets of numbers. Use it to find the next number.

Find the next number in these series.

2, _____ 4, _____ 6, _____
+ 2   + 2   + 2
× 2   × 2

1. Look at the first two numbers. How do they relate?
   2 + 2 = 4.
   2 × 2 = 4.
   Test both patterns on the next set of numbers.

2. Look at the second two numbers. How do they relate?
   4 + 2 = 6.
   4 × 2 = 8, not 6.
   The pattern must be + 2.

3. Use the pattern to find the next number.
   6 + 2 = 8.
   The next number must be 8.

Find the next number in these series.

1. 5, 7, 9, _____11_____

2. 9, 12, 15, _____

3. 2, 6, 18, _____

4. 3, 10, 17, _____

5. 2, 6, 10, _____

6. 5, 20, 80, _____

7. 5, 10, 15, _____

8. 7, 11, 15, _____

9. 2, 4, 6, _____

10. 3, 12, 48, _____

Using a Multiplication Table

A multiplication table shows multiplication facts. The numbers above and to the left of the double lines are the numbers that are multiplied. The numbers inside the squares are the answers, or **products**.

The row for 2 and the column for 3 cross at 6.
This means that $3 \times 2 = 6$.
It also means that $2 \times 3 = 6$.
It also means that $6 \div 3 = 2$ and $6 \div 2 = 3$.

Finish the table to show all the basic multiplication facts. Then use the table to answer the questions that follow.

×	0	1	2	3	4	5	6	7	8	9
0	0	0	0	0						
1	0	1	2	3						
2	0	2	4	6						
3	0	3	6	9						
4										
5						30				
6										
7					35					
8				24						72
9							63			

1. The table shows two different ways to get 2 for an answer. What are they?

    _____ × _____ = 2   _____ × _____ = 2

2. The table shows that $8 \times 3 = 24$. Use the table to find these answers.

    $24 \div 3 =$ _____ $24 \div 8 =$ _____ $3 \times$ _____ $= 24$

Use the multiplication table to find the answers.

3. $2 \times 4 =$ 8

4. $3 \times 4 =$ _____

5. $4 \times 4 =$ _____

6. $5 \times 4 =$ _____

7. $6 \times 4 =$ _____

8. $7 \times 4 =$ _____

9. $8 \times$ _____ $= 8$

10. $8 \times$ _____ $= 16$

11. $8 \times$ _____ $= 24$

12. $6 \times 5 =$ _____

13. $30 \div 6 =$ _____

14. $30 \div 5 =$ _____

15. $7 \times$ _____ $= 49$

16. $49 \div 7 =$ _____

17. $9 \times$ _____ $= 72$

18. $72 \div 8 =$ _____

19. $72 \div 9 =$ _____

20. $54 \div$ _____ $= 9$

Fill in the missing × or ÷ in these number sentences.

21. 2 __÷__ $2 = 1$

22. 2 _____ $6 = 12$

23. 2 _____ $9 = 18$

24. 18 _____ $2 = 9$

25. 12 _____ $6 = 2$

26. 20 _____ $4 = 5$

27. 6 _____ $7 = 42$

28. 42 _____ $7 = 6$

29. 3 _____ $1 = 3$

30. 3 _____ $6 = 18$

31. 5 _____ $7 = 35$

32. 7 _____ $7 = 49$

33. 45 _____ $9 = 5$

34. 56 _____ $8 = 7$

35. 8 _____ $7 = 56$

Write two division sentences for each multiplication sentence.

36. $3 \times 6 = 18$ $18 \div 3 = 6$ $18 \div 6 = 3$

37. $9 \times 8 = 72$ _____ _____

38. $5 \times 7 = 35$ _____ _____

39. $4 \times 3 = 12$ _____ _____

Adding and Multiplying Using a Calculator

Using a calculator can cut down the time it takes to find the answers to math problems. There are many kinds of calculators on the market today. Most calculators have at least the keys shown here.

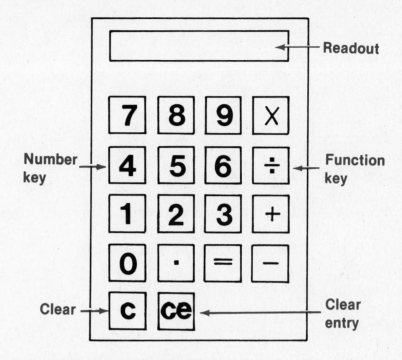

The **readout** window, at the top, is where the answer shows.

The **number keys,** at the left, are for punching in the numbers that you're working with.

The **function keys,** at the right, tell the calculator what to do.

$\times$ is used to **multiply.** $+$ is used to **add.**

$\div$ is used to **divide.** $-$ is used to **subtract.**

$=$ means equals.   Press this key when you've told the calculator what to do and you want the answer.

c means clear.   When you press this key, everything in the calculator is erased, and you can start over.

ce means clear entry.   When you press this key, you erase only the last number you put into the calculator. Not all calculators have this key.

Numbers can be added or multiplied in any order with a calculator. However, before starting, press the C button. This will clear out the last problem.

Examples

A. Add 789 and 234.

Press 7 , 8 , 9 .

Press + .

Press 2 , 3 , 4 .

Press = . Read the answer and write it down.

Press C before starting the next problem.

B. Multiply 231 × 46.

Press 2 , 3 , 1 .

Press × .

Press 4 , 6 .

Press = . Read the answer and write it down.

Press C before starting the next problem.

> **MATH HINT**
>
> Some calculators have a CCE button. It means *clear* or *clear entry*. To clear *everything* out, push the button *twice*. To clear only the last number you put in, push the button once. *Clear entry* comes in handy when you enter the wrong number by mistake.

Practice

Work each problem on a calculator. Write your answer. See if you get the same answer when you do the problem in reverse order.

1. $548 + 34 + 290 + 14 =$ _____

2. $762 \times 59 =$ _____

3. $678 + 432 + 56 + 903 =$ _____

4. $24 \times 32 \times 12 =$ _____

5. $19 \times 43 + 89 =$ _____

6. $870 + 43 + 12 \times 4 =$ _____

Problem Solving

Solve the following problems using a calculator.

7. The Elton Heights area has 4 communities. Astor Village has 12,890 people. Cape Ridge has 13,456. Rainbow Hills has 15,674, and Victoria Creek has 16,724 people. What is the total population of Elton Heights? _____

8. Linc collects baseball cards. He has 456 baseball cards in his collection. For his birthday, he received 32 more cards. What is the total number of cards he now has? _____

9. Alma is reading a book that has 22 chapters. Each chapter has 35 pages. How many pages does the book have? _____

10. Catalina drives 5 days a week from home to school and back. The trip is 16 miles each way. How many miles does she drive each week to school and home? _____

Subtracting and Dividing Using a Calculator

You can add or multiply in any order with a calculator. However, when you divide or subtract, it is important to punch in the right number first.

Example

You know that $6 \div 3 = 2$.
Try it on the calculator.

     $\underline{\quad 2 \quad}$

Now see what happens when you punch in the numbers the other way. You get the wrong answer.

3 ÷ 6 = $\underline{\quad .5 \quad}$

Practice

Work each problem on a calculator. Write your answer. Check by doing the problem again.

1. $2,080 \div 32 =$ _____

2. $3,738 - 42 =$ _____

3. $756,231 - 325,610 =$ _____

4. $211,896 \div 324 =$ _____

5. $987,564 - 321,897 =$ _____

6. $556,668 \div 987 =$ _____

Solve the following problems using a calculator.

7. Lester had 213 CDs in his collection. He gave his sister 22 of them. How many does he have left?

     _____

8. Jackie weighs 182 pounds. She went on a diet and lost 53 pounds. How much does she weigh now?

     _____

9. Mr. and Mrs. Morez are planning their wedding anniversary party. They invited 189 people. If each table seats 9 people, how many tables will they need?

     _____

Use the information from Problem 9 to help you answer the following problem:

10. Lucy's flower shop will provide table centerpieces for the Morez's anniversary party. If Lucy has 462 flowers to work with, how many flowers can she use for each table's centerpiece?

     _____

Problem Solving—Multiplication and Division

You have been solving word problems in the previous lessons. You should remember that these problems can be solved if you keep in mind the following steps:

Step 1 Read the problem and underline the key words. These words will usually relate to some mathematics reasoning computation.

Step 2 Make a plan to solve the problem. Ask yourself, Should I add, subtract, multiply, divide, round, or compare? You may have to do more than one operation for the same problem. You may also be able to estimate your answer.

Step 3 Find the solution. Use your math knowledge to find your answer.

Step 4 Check the answer. Ask yourself, Is the answer reasonable? Did you find what you were asked for?

Here are some key words for multiplication and division:

Multiplication	**Division**
product	quotient
times	per
how much	for each
of	average
apiece	shared
multiplied by	

Examples

A. Chicken costs $3 a pound on sale. Nancita bought 8 pounds of chicken. How much did she spend?

Step 1 Determine how much Nancita spent. The key words are **how much.**

Step 2 The key words indicate which operation should occur—multiplication.

Step 3 Find the solution. $3 \times 8 = 24

Step 4 Check the answer. Does it make sense that 8 pounds of chicken at $3 each would cost $24? Yes, the answer is reasonable.

B. Lance works as a packer. He packed 128 boxes in 8 hours. How many boxes did he pack per hour?

Step 1   Determine how many boxes Lance packed per hour. The key words are **per hour.**

Step 2   The key words indicate which operation should occur—division.

Step 3   Find the solution. $128 \div 8 = 16$ boxes per hour

Step 4   Check the answer. Does it make sense that Lance packed 16 boxes per hour to reach a total of 128 boxes at the end of 8 hours? Yes, the answer is reasonable.

Practice

Solve the following problems.

1. Mr. Yoshimura has a barbershop. He can give 3 haircuts an hour. How many haircuts can he give in 7 hours?   _____

2. Ms. Parker can type 5 pages an hour. How many pages can she type in 4 hours?   _____

3. Kara paid $124 for 31 corsages. How much did each corsage cost?   _____

4. Philip paid $10.90 for gasoline. If he got 10 gallons, how much did each gallon cost?   _____

5. Alex has taken 3 courses in math; 10 courses in science; 14 courses in general studies. If each course is worth 3 credits apiece, what are the total credits he has earned?   _____

6. Danny can take dictation at 80 words a minute. How many words can he take at the end of 10 minutes?   _____

7. Sasha leased a car for 6 months. The rate was $150 each month. How much did her lease cost at the end of that time period?   _____

Posttest

Multiply.

1. $2 \times 3 =$ _____   2. $8 \times 3 =$ _____   3. $7 \times 3 =$ _____   4. $9 \times 5 =$ _____

5. $\begin{array}{r} 6 \\ \times\, 5 \\ \hline \end{array}$ 6. $\begin{array}{r} 8 \\ \times\, 8 \\ \hline \end{array}$ 7. $\begin{array}{r} 9 \\ \times\, 9 \\ \hline \end{array}$ 8. $\begin{array}{r} 7 \\ \times\, 8 \\ \hline \end{array}$

Divide.

9. $16 \div 2 =$ _____   10. $18 \div 9 =$ _____   11. $27 \div 3 =$ _____   12. $49 \div 7 =$ _____

13. $63 \div 7 =$ _____   14. $40 \div 5 =$ _____   15. $30 \div 6 =$ _____   16. $54 \div 6 =$ _____

Write four different number sentences using 7, 63, and 9.

17. _____   _____   _____   _____

Complete these number sentences.

18. $2 \times 3 =$ _____   19. $8 \div 2 =$ _____   20. $21 \div 3 =$ _____   21. $18 \div 2 =$ _____

22. _____ $\times 4 = 4$ 23. _____ $\times 5 = 35$ 24. _____ $\times 6 = 36$ 25. _____ $\div 8 = 5$

26. $32 \div$ _____ $= 8$ 27. $64 \div$ _____ $= 8$ 28. $9 \div$ _____ $= 3$ 29. $4 \times$ _____ $= 20$

Problem Solving

Circle the letter of the correct answer.

30. Ms. Zlata made $63. She worked 9 hours. How much did she make per hour?

    a. $54   **b.** $48   **c.** $7

31. Mr. Pattanasi bought 4 books for $5 each. How much did he spend in all?

    a. $20   **b.** $30   **c.** $9

Multiplying

Multiply.

1. $\begin{array}{r} 36 \\ \times\ 2 \\ \hline \end{array}$
2. $\begin{array}{r} 49 \\ \times\ 5 \\ \hline \end{array}$
3. $\begin{array}{r} 87 \\ \times\ 9 \\ \hline \end{array}$
4. $\begin{array}{r} 206 \\ \times\ \ \ 3 \\ \hline \end{array}$

5. $\begin{array}{r} 478 \\ \times\ \ \ 5 \\ \hline \end{array}$
6. $\begin{array}{r} 913 \\ \times\ \ \ 6 \\ \hline \end{array}$
7. $\begin{array}{r} 345 \\ \times\ \ \ 8 \\ \hline \end{array}$
8. $\begin{array}{r} 217 \\ \times\ \ \ 7 \\ \hline \end{array}$

9. $4 \times 3 \times 6 =$ _____
10. $9 \times 5 \times 7 =$ _____
11. $4 \times 8 \times 2 =$ _____

12. $3 \times 4 \times 6 =$ _____
13. $8 \times 7 \times 5 =$ _____
14. $6 \times 9 \times 2 =$ _____

15. $50 \times 5 =$ _____
16. $70 \times 200 =$ _____
17. $600 \times 500 =$ _____

18. $60 \times 3 =$ _____
19. $500 \times 9 =$ _____
20. $8,000 \times 50 =$ _____

Estimate the answer. Then find the exact answer.

21. $\begin{array}{r} 75 \\ \times\ 32 \\ \hline \end{array}$ Estimate

22. $\begin{array}{r} 4,176 \\ \times\ \ \ \ 57 \\ \hline \end{array}$ Estimate

23.   1 1 7   Estimate   **24.**   2 , 5 9 6   Estimate
     × 5 0 3   ×   3 4 7
               _____   _____

Multiply.

25.   7 8   **26.**   4 7   **27.**   6 3
    × 5 2   × 2 5   × 5 8

28.   8 7 4   **29.**   5 3 8   **30.**   1 , 6 8 3
    ×   4 6   ×   8 2   ×   4 6

31.   4 5 3   **32.**   7 , 8 3 6   **33.**   4 , 9 6 1
    × 5 0 9   ×   6 9 7   ×   3 7 0

Problem Solving

Solve the following problems.

34. Six workers each made $9 an hour for 6 hours. How much did they make in all?   _____

35. Barb's rent is $235 a month. How much rent does she pay at the end of a year?   _____

36. There were 237 people on the plane to San Juan. Each ticket cost $345. What was the total cost of all the tickets?   _____

Multiplying by One-Digit Numbers

When you multiply a number by a one-digit number, follow these steps:

Step 1   Multiply the number in the ones place.

Step 2   Multiply the number in the tens place.

Step 3   Continue to multiply the numbers in each place value position.

> **MATH HINT**
>
> The **multiplicand** is the number that is multiplied by another number. The **multiplier** is the number that multiplies another number.

Examples

A. Mary bought 3 dresses. They cost $36 each. How much did she spend in all? Multiply 36 × 3.

Step 1 $3 \times 6 = 18$. $18 = 1$ ten $+ 8$ ones.

$$\begin{array}{r} \overset{1}{3}6 \\ \times\ \ 3 \\ \hline 8 \end{array}$$

Put 8 ones in the ones place in the answer.
Put 1 ten above the tens column.

Step 2 $3 \times 3 = 9$. 9 tens $+ 1$ ten $= 10$ tens.

$$\begin{array}{r} \overset{1}{3}6 \\ \times\ \ 3 \\ \hline 108 \end{array}$$

Put 10 tens in the tens place in the answer.

The answer has 10 tens and 8 ones.
The answer is $108.

B. Josef made $245 a week for 4 weeks. How much did he make over the four weeks? Multiply 245 × 4.

Step 1 $4 \times 5 = 20$. $20 = 2$ tens $+ 0$ ones.

$$\begin{array}{r} 2\overset{2}{4}5 \\ \times\ \ \ 4 \\ \hline 0 \end{array}$$

Put 0 ones in the ones place in the answer.
Put 2 tens above the tens column.

Step 2 $4 \times 4 = 16$ tens.
16 tens $+ 2$ tens $= 18$ tens.
18 tens $= 1$ hundred $+ 8$ tens.

$$\begin{array}{r} \overset{1}{2}\overset{2}{4}5 \\ \times\ \ \ 4 \\ \hline 80 \end{array}$$

Put 8 tens in the tens place in the answer.
Put 1 hundred above the hundreds column.

Step 3 $4 \times 2 = 8$ hundreds.
          4 hundreds + 1 hundred = 9 hundreds.

$$\begin{array}{r} \overset{1 \; 2}{2\,4\,5} \\ \times \quad 4 \\ \hline 9\,8\,0 \end{array}$$

Put 9 hundreds in the hundreds place in the answer.

The answer has 9 hundreds + 8 tens + 0 ones.
The answer is $980.

Practice

Multiply.

1. $\begin{array}{r} 3\,3 \\ \times \; 4 \\ \hline \end{array}$

2. $\begin{array}{r} 4\,1 \\ \times \; 7 \\ \hline \end{array}$

3. $\begin{array}{r} 5\,2 \\ \times \; 5 \\ \hline \end{array}$

4. $\begin{array}{r} 4\,9 \\ \times \; 6 \\ \hline \end{array}$

5. $\begin{array}{r} 5\,7 \\ \times \; 8 \\ \hline \end{array}$

6. $\begin{array}{r} 6\,8 \\ \times \; 9 \\ \hline \end{array}$

7. $\begin{array}{r} 7\,3 \\ \times \; 7 \\ \hline \end{array}$

8. $\begin{array}{r} 9\,2 \\ \times \; 3 \\ \hline \end{array}$

9. $\begin{array}{r} 3\,8 \\ \times \; 5 \\ \hline \end{array}$

10. $\begin{array}{r} 9\,7 \\ \times \; 4 \\ \hline \end{array}$

11. $\begin{array}{r} 6\,4\,2 \\ \times \quad 2 \\ \hline \end{array}$

12. $\begin{array}{r} 2\,2\,4 \\ \times \quad 3 \\ \hline \end{array}$

13. $138 \times 5 =$ _____

14. $368 \times 2 =$ _____

Problem Solving

Solve the following problems.

15. Eddie makes $46 a day. How much does he make in a 5-day week?

_____

16. Vera pays $138 a month for her car. How much does she pay in 6 months?

_____

17. If potatoes cost 43¢ a pound, how much would 4 pounds cost?

_____

18. Jerry makes $980 a month. How much does he make in 7 months?

_____

Multiplying Three Numbers

When you multiply more than two numbers, you can multiply in any order. You can multiply the first two numbers, then multiply the last—or in any order you choose.

---------- **Example** ----------

Mr. Herrero has 8 people working for him. He pays them $6 an hour. On Monday, the crew worked for 7 hours. How much did Mr. Herrero have to pay his workers?

Write the numbers this way.
$8 \times 6 \times 7 = ?$

Multiply any two of the numbers.

Then multiply the answer by the third number.

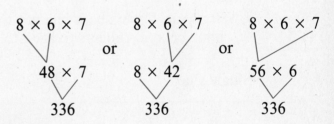

---------- **Practice** ----------

Multiply.

1. $2 \times 4 \times 6 =$ _____

2. $3 \times 6 \times 7 =$ _____

3. $4 \times 6 \times 8 =$ _____

4. $5 \times 3 \times 8 =$ _____

5. $4 \times 7 \times 9 =$ _____

6. $7 \times 3 \times 2 =$ _____

Problem Solving

Solve the problems.

10. Rob and Ted rented a cabin. They each paid $16 a day. They stayed for seven days. What did they spend in all?

_____

11. The library charges 5¢ a day for each book returned late. Ira took out 3 books. He was 4 days late in returning them. How much did he have to pay?

_____

Comparing Recreation Costs

The YMCA has a track, a gym, a swimming pool, and a
weight room. Members can use them free. Others must buy
a guest pass. Members also get lower rates on classes.

Here is what the YMCA charges. Read the table. Then
answer the questions.

Family Plan

$80 a year. Covers both parents and all children through high
school; college students to age 21.

Single Plan

Men	$75
Women	65
Children Grades 1–8	25
High school and college	35

Guest Passes

Adults	$3
Grades 1–8	1
High school and college	2

Classes (7 weeks each)	Members	Nonmembers
Yoga	$18	$25
Dance	15	30
Racquetball	18	35
Fitness	10	20

---

1. Emma is interested in joining with a single plan. What will a
   single plan cost her for one year? _____

2. How much is it to buy an adult guest pass every week for a
   year? (There are 52 weeks in a year.) _____

3. Regina uses the Y once a week. How much can she save with the single plan? _____

4. There are 4 high-school children in the Bono family. They use the Y. Their parents do not. Which costs them less, the family plan or the single plan? _____

5. Harvey just wants to play racquetball. What will he pay if he signs up for classes 7 times during the year and is not a member? _____

6. What does a member pay for racquetball classes 7 times a year? _____

7. Add the cost of the single plan for men to the answer in #6. Should Harvey join the Y? _____

Multiplying Numbers That End in Zero

When multiplying numbers that end in zero, follow these steps:

Step 1   Count the number of zeros.

Step 2   Put that number of zeros in the answer.

Step 3   Then multiply the numbers that are not zeros.

Step 4   Put that answer in front of the zeros for the final answer.

Examples

A. Mr. Subi sold 40 TV sets for $90 each.
How much money did he take in?

```
       4 0     1 zero
  ×      9 0     1 zero
  $ 3 , 6 0 0   2 zeros
```

B. Margie sold 20 sweaters for $50 each.
How much money did she take in?

```
       2 0     1 zero
  ×      5 0     1 zero
  $ 1 , 0 0 0   2 zeros
```

C. The order department at SuperSaver fills 3,000 orders a week.
How many orders are filled in 12 weeks?

```
    3 , 0 0 0   3 zeros
  ×      1 2    0 zeros
   3 6 , 0 0 0  3 zeros
```

Practice

Multiply.

1. 4 0 × 5	**2.** 3 0 × 2	**3.** 6 0 × 4	**4.** 5 0 × 5
5. 7 0 × 3	**6.** 9 0 × 4	**7.** 8 0 × 7	**8.** 2 0 × 9

9. $\begin{array}{r} 1\,0 \\ \times\ 6 \\ \hline \end{array}$ 10. $\begin{array}{r} 5\,0 \\ \times\ 6 \\ \hline \end{array}$ 11. $\begin{array}{r} 4\,0 \\ \times\ 8 \\ \hline \end{array}$ 12. $\begin{array}{r} 3\,0 \\ \times\ 7 \\ \hline \end{array}$

13. $\begin{array}{r} 2\,0 \\ \times 4\,0 \\ \hline \end{array}$ 14. $\begin{array}{r} 4\,0 \\ \times 6\,0 \\ \hline \end{array}$ 15. $\begin{array}{r} 5\,0 \\ \times 6\,0 \\ \hline \end{array}$ 16. $\begin{array}{r} 4\,0 \\ \times 9\,0 \\ \hline \end{array}$

17. $\begin{array}{r} 6\,0 \\ \times 7\,0 \\ \hline \end{array}$ 18. $\begin{array}{r} 6\,0 \\ \times 6\,0 \\ \hline \end{array}$ 19. $\begin{array}{r} 2\,0\,0 \\ \times\ \ 4\,0 \\ \hline \end{array}$ 20. $\begin{array}{r} 3\,0\,0 \\ \times 2\,0\,0 \\ \hline \end{array}$

21. $\begin{array}{r} 8\,0\,0 \\ \times\ \ 6\,0 \\ \hline \end{array}$ 22. $\begin{array}{r} 1{,}0\,0\,0 \\ \times\ \ \ \ 1\,4 \\ \hline \end{array}$ 23. $\begin{array}{r} 8{,}0\,0\,0 \\ \times\ \ \ \ 3\,0 \\ \hline \end{array}$ 24. $\begin{array}{r} 2{,}0\,0\,0 \\ \times\ \ \ 5\,0\,0 \\ \hline \end{array}$

Problem Solving

Solve these problems.

25. Forty people paid $50 each to take a class. How much did they
pay in all? _____

26. Stephen bought 40 acres of land for $300 an acre. What was his
total cost for the land? _____

27. Thirty people purchased movie tickets for $5 each. How much
did they pay in all? _____

28. Hadrian's sold 50 wedding rings for $400 each. How much did
the rings cost altogether? _____

29. Five hundred families joined the food co-op. Each family paid
$100. How much did the families pay in all? _____

Finding Weekly Pay

Ernesto Vega's time card is shown below. Find Ernesto's gross pay—that is, pay before taxes. Complete the time card. Multiply the hours worked each day by the pay per hour to find the gross pay. Add amounts 1–6 to find the total pay for the week. Then, answer the questions below.

Vega, E.	In	Out	In	Out	Hours per day	Pay per hour	Gross pay
Monday	8:00	12:00	1:00	4:00	7	$8	1. _____
Tuesday	8:30	11:30	1:00	4:00	6	$8	2. _____
Wednesday	8:00	12:30	1:30	5:00	8	$8	3. _____
Thursday	7:30	12:00	1:30	5:00	8	$8	4. _____
Friday	8:00	12:00	1:00	4:00	7	$8	5. _____
Saturday	9:00	1:00			4	$12	6. _____
						Total	7. _____

8. If Ernesto made the same pay each week, what would he make in a month? (There are 4 weeks in a month.) _____

9. If Ernesto worked for 8 hours on Saturday, how much would he make? _____

10. Next January, Ernesto will start making $9 an hour. If he works 40 hours a week, what will his gross pay be each week? _____

 Each month? _____

Multiplying by Two-Digit Numbers

When multiplying a number by two-digit numbers, you should follow these steps:

Step 1 Multiply by the digit in the ones place.

Step 2 Then multiply by the digit in the tens place.

Step 3 Add the two numbers to get the answer.

Examples

A. Lorna saves $56 a month. How much does she save a year?
$56 \times 12 = ?$

> **MATH HINT**
>
> **R**emember: The **multiplier** is the number that multiplies another number; the number that is being multiplied is the **multiplicand**.

To find the answer, follow these steps.

Step 1 $56 \times 2 = 112$ ———————

$$
\begin{array}{r}
5\,6 \quad \text{multiplicand} \\
\times \quad 1\,2 \quad \text{multiplier} \\
\hline
1\,1\,2 \\
5\,6\,0 \\
\hline
6\,7\,2
\end{array}
$$

Step 2 $56 \times 10 = 560$ ———————

Step 3 $112 + 560 = 672$ ———————

B. Nicki pays $235 a month to rent three rooms in a house. What is his rent for 18 months?
$235 \times 18 = ?$

$$
\begin{array}{r}
2\,3\,5 \\
\times \quad 1\,8 \\
\hline
1{,}8\,8\,0 \\
2{,}3\,5\,0 \\
\hline
4{,}2\,3\,0
\end{array}
$$

Step 1 8×235 ————————→ $1,880$

Step 2 10×235 ————————→ $2,350$

Step 3 $1,880 + 2,350$ ————————→ $4,230$

Multiply.

1. 68
    × 24

2. 86
    × 42

3. 73
    × 31

4. 532
    × 24

5. 465
    × 13

6. 636
    × 35

7. 888
    × 22

8. 236
    × 73

9. 569
    × 46

10. 4,632
     ×   27

11. 2,843
     ×   34

12. 6,045
     ×   52

Problem Solving

Solve the following problems.

13. Juana pays $45 a month for medical insurance. What does her insurance cost for a year? _____

14. Emil saves $15 a week. How much does he save in a year? (52 weeks in a year) _____

15. Matty makes $236 a week. What is her yearly pay? _____

16. Fifty-eight people took the bus to New York City. Each ticket cost $125. How much did the riders pay in all? _____

17. Danny sold 14 cars for $1,999 each. How much did he make? _____

Finding Hospital Costs

Gloria Kane and Ester Mitchell both had their babies at Central
Hospital. Gloria belonged to the Central Neighborhood Health
Plan. It lowered her costs. Ester paid the full rate.

Complete these bills. Then answer the questions below.

Gloria Kane
Mother's bill

Room $300/day for 3 days	1.	_____
Labor room	2.	$250
Delivery room and supplies	3.	$ 95
Lab	4.	$ 43
Central supply	5.	$ 21
Telephone $5/day for 3 days	6.	_____
Total for mother	7.	_____

Baby's bill

Nursery $225/day for 3 days	8.	_____
Lab	9.	$105
Total for baby	10.	_____
Total for mother and baby	11.	_____

Ester Mitchell
Mother's bill

Room $425/day for 3 days	12.	_____
Labor room	13.	$200
Delivery room supplies	14.	$758
Anesthesia nurse	15.	$440
Anesthesia supplies	16.	$145
Pharmacy	17.	$298
Lab	18.	$275
Central supply	19.	$115
Telephone $6/day for 3 days	20.	_____
Total for mother	21.	_____

Baby's bill

Nursery $375/day for 3 days	22.	_____
Pharmacy	23.	$ 35
Lab	24.	$520
Total for baby	25.	_____
Total for mother and baby	26.	_____

27. What did Gloria pay in all for hospital room, labor room,
and delivery room? _____

28. What did Ester pay in all for hospital room, labor room,
and delivery room? _____

Multiplying by Three-Digit Numbers

When multiplying a number by a three-digit number, you should follow these steps:

Step 1   Multiply by the digit in the ones place.
Step 2   Multiply by the digit in the tens place.
Step 3   Then multiply by the digit in the hundreds place.
Step 4   Add all three numbers to get the answer.

Example

The Hotel Belmont has 235 rooms. Each room costs $153 a year to heat. What does it cost to heat all the rooms for a year?

Step 1 $3 \times 235 = 705$

Step 2 $50 \times 235 = 11,750$

Step 3 $100 \times 235 = 23,500$

Step 4 $705 + 11,750 + 23,500 = 35,955$

```
    2 3 5
  × 1 5 3
      7 0 5
  1 1 , 7 5 0
  2 3 , 5 0 0
  3 5 , 9 5 5
```

Practice

Multiply.

1. 456
    × 127

2. 568
    × 224

3. 608
    × 252

4. 589
    × 236

5. 944
    × 538

6. 743
    × 269

Multiplying With Zeros in the Multiplier

When you have a **zero** in the multiplier, or bottom number, you can skip that place in multiplication. Every answer in that place would be zero.

Example

Mrs. Rojak retired exactly 3 years—156 weeks—ago. Since then she has been getting $102 a week from the retirement fund. How much money has Mrs. Rojak received in all?

Step 1 Multiply by ones.
$156 \times 2 = 312$

Step 2 There is a zero in the tens place. When a zero appears in the multiplier, there is no need to multiply. Zero times any number equals zero.

Step 3 Multiply by the hundreds.
$156 \times 100 = 15,600$

Step 4 Add the numbers.
$312 + 15,600 = 15,912$

$$\begin{array}{r} 1\,5\,6 \\ \times\,1\,0\,2 \\ \hline 3\,1\,2 \\ 1\,5,6\,0\,0 \\ \hline 1\,5,9\,1\,2 \end{array}$$

> **MATH HINT**
>
> The bottom number is the **multiplier.**

Practice

Multiply.

1. $\begin{array}{r} 5\,6\,9 \\ \times\,2\,0\,4 \\ \hline \end{array}$

2. $\begin{array}{r} 6\,7\,8 \\ \times\,7\,0\,3 \\ \hline \end{array}$

3. $\begin{array}{r} 5\,5\,5 \\ \times\,1\,0\,9 \\ \hline \end{array}$

4. $\begin{array}{r} 8,9\,1\,2 \\ \times\quad 5\,0\,6 \\ \hline \end{array}$

5. $\begin{array}{r} 3,4\,2\,9 \\ \times\quad 8\,0\,8 \\ \hline \end{array}$

6. $\begin{array}{r} 9,0\,4\,9 \\ \times\quad 8\,7\,0 \\ \hline \end{array}$

Estimating in Multiplication

To estimate an answer in multiplication, first round the given numbers. Estimating is helpful when you don't need to know the exact amount, since you can more easily multiply rounded numbers.

Examples

A. Estimate 235 × 18 = ?

Round 235 to the nearest hundred → 200
Round 18 to the nearest ten   → 20

Now you can multiply more easily.

```
    2 0 0
×      2 0
  4 , 0 0 0
```

B. Cord earns $42 a day. How much would he earn if he works 21 days this month? Estimate your answer.

Round $42 to the nearest ten → $40
Round 21 to the nearest ten → 20

```
  $ 4 0
×   2 0
$ 8 0 0
```

Practice

Estimate the answer. Then find the exact answer.

1.	4 9	Estimate	2.	6 8	Estimate	3.	5 0 7	Estimate
	× 6 3			× 3 7			× 4 3	

4. 774   Estimate   **5.** 475   Estimate   **6.** 3,562   Estimate
    × 69   × 31   × 48

_____   _____   _____

7. 4,746   Estimate   **8.** 894   Estimate   **9.** 627   Estimate
    × 92   ×146   ×593

_____   _____   _____

10. 5,724   Estimate   **11.** 8,490   Estimate   **12.** 4,682   Estimate
    × 308   × 527   × 246

_____   _____   _____

Problem Solving

Solve the following problems. Estimate the answer; then give the exact answer.

13. Each of 5 workers made $6 an hour for 8 hours. How much did they make altogether?

Estimate Answer

_____

Exact Answer

_____

14. Mr. Sanchez was hurt on the job. He got payments of $145 a week for 52 weeks. How much money did he get in all?

Estimate Answer

_____

Exact Answer

_____

Problem Solving—Two Operations

Keep in mind the following steps when solving multiplication problems. Remember, when you are planning to solve a problem, you may have to do more than one operation.

Step 1   Read the problem and underline the key words. These words will usually relate to some mathematics reasoning computation.

Step 2   Make a plan to solve the problem. Ask yourself, Should I add, subtract, multiply, divide, round, or compare? You may have to do more than one operation for the same problem. You may also be able to estimate your answer.

Step 3   Find the solution. Use your math knowledge to find your answer.

Step 4   Check the answer. Ask yourself, Is the answer reasonable? Did you find what you were asked for?

Here are some key words for multiplication and addition:

Multiplication	Addition
product	altogether
how much	both
of	increase
apiece	sum
multiplied by	total
	together
	in all

Example

Simon earns $6 an hour for painting. He worked three different painting jobs this week. On Job 1, he worked 9 hours; Job 2, he worked 4 hours; and on Job 3, he worked 5 hours. How much did he earn altogether this week?

Step 1   Determine how much Simon earned altogether. The key words are **altogether** and **how much.**

Step 2   The key words indicate which operations should occur—addition and multiplication. You first have to add the number of hours he worked. Then, multiply the hours worked by his hourly rate.

Step 3 Find the solution.

9 + 4 + 5 = 18 total hours worked $6 × 18 = $108

Step 4 Check the answer. Does it make sense that 18 hours worked at $6 an hour comes to $108? Yes, the answer is reasonable.

Practice

Solve the following problems.

1. Frances plans to take 9 senior citizens, 2 children, and 1 adult to a community play. The tickets cost $1 for children, $2 for seniors, and $3 for adults. How much money will she have to collect altogether?

2. Barry has a paper route. He has 35 customers who pay him weekly and 10 customers who pay him monthly. The delivery cost is $4 weekly or $15 monthly. How much does he collect in all at the end of the month?

3. Northside Community College charges $50 for each credit hour of class. Susan needs a 4-credit hour class in History and a 3-credit hour class in English to graduate. How much will it cost Susan to take these classes?

4. The City Zoo has 5 new elephants. It costs $575 a month to feed each elephant. How much does it cost to feed the elephants for one year?

5. Gracie has 3 children who attend the day care center. The cost is $4 a day for each child. Her children go to day care only 3 days a week. At the end of one week, how much does she pay the day care center?

6

Posttest

Multiply.

1. $\begin{array}{r} 46 \\ \times\ \ 3 \\ \hline \end{array}$

2. $\begin{array}{r} 98 \\ \times\ \ 5 \\ \hline \end{array}$

3. $\begin{array}{r} 87 \\ \times\ \ 9 \\ \hline \end{array}$

4. $\begin{array}{r} 143 \\ \times\ \ \ \ 7 \\ \hline \end{array}$

5. $\begin{array}{r} 465 \\ \times\ \ \ \ 6 \\ \hline \end{array}$

6. $\begin{array}{r} 709 \\ \times\ \ \ \ 7 \\ \hline \end{array}$

7. $\begin{array}{r} 843 \\ \times\ \ \ \ 8 \\ \hline \end{array}$

8. $\begin{array}{r} 1,942 \\ \times\ \ \ \ \ \ 5 \\ \hline \end{array}$

9. $8 \times 3 \times 5 = $ _____

10. $2 \times 7 \times 6 = $ _____

11. $5 \times 5 \times 9 = $ _____

12. $5 \times 4 \times 8 = $ _____

13. $6 \times 3 \times 9 = $ _____

14. $2 \times 7 \times 4 = $ _____

15. $40 \times 5 = $ _____

16. $90 \times 6 = $ _____

17. $500 \times 6 = $ _____

18. $300 \times 20 = $ _____

19. $4,000 \times 70 = $ _____

20. $2,000 \times 400 = $ _____

Estimate the answer. Then find the exact answer.

21. $\begin{array}{r} 67 \\ \times 14 \\ \hline \end{array}$ Estimate

   _____

22. $\begin{array}{r} 894 \\ \times\ \ 26 \\ \hline \end{array}$ Estimate

   _____

23. $\begin{array}{r} 3,607 \\ \times\ \ \ \ \ 48 \\ \hline \end{array}$ Estimate

   _____

24. $\begin{array}{r} 583 \\ \times 124 \\ \hline \end{array}$ Estimate

   _____

25. $\begin{array}{r} 888 \\ \times 209 \\ \hline \end{array}$ Estimate

   _____

26. $\begin{array}{r} 5,487 \\ \times\ \ \ \ 361 \\ \hline \end{array}$ Estimate

   _____

Multiply.

27.   2 4
       × 2 3

28.   7 8 2
       ×   4 8

29.   2 , 3 5 9
       ×   7 8

30.   4 0 9
       × 1 6 7

31.   8 , 3 0 2
       ×   4 8 9

32.   5 , 8 1 4
       ×   2 9 3

33.   7 , 1 3 1
       ×   5 0 9

34.   4 , 5 9 3
       ×   4 0 2

35.   4 , 9 1 7
       ×   7 2 0

Problem Solving

Solve the following problems.

36. Emily and Vicki rented a car. Each had to pay $13 a day. They kept the car for 2 days. How much did Emily and Vicki pay altogether?   _____

37. The moving company charged $10 an hour for each mover on the crew. When the McFarlands moved, they needed a crew of 4. It took 5 hours. What was the total bill?   _____

38. There are 678 students at the Music Center. Each one pays $355 a year. What do the students pay in all?   _____

39. Fifty-eight people took the bus to New York City. Each ticket cost $125. How much did the riders pay in all?   _____

40. Danny sold 14 cars for $1,999 each. How much did he make?   _____

UNIT

7

Dividing

Pretest

Divide. Show any remainders.

1. 6)49

2. 4)35

3. 8)90

4. 31)95

5. 28)89

6. 7)572

7. 4)679

8. 19)843

9. 27)385

10. 84)9,743

11. 68)8,509

12. 72)8,937

13. $105\overline{)72,895}$ **14.** $214\overline{)13,698}$ **15.** $337\overline{)13,820}$

16. $472\overline{)63,729}$ **17.** $389\overline{)84,030}$ **18.** $441\overline{)23,810}$

Estimate the answers.

19. $23\overline{)6,719}$ Between _____ and _____   **20.** $39\overline{)9,732}$ Between _____ and _____

21. $102\overline{)567}$ Between _____ and _____   **22.** $814\overline{)19,563}$ Between _____ and _____

Find the answers. Check by multiplying.

23. $7\overline{)596}$ **24.** $87\overline{)68,956}$ **25.** $357\overline{)7,140}$

Problem Solving

Solve the following problems.

26. Christine worked for 3 months. She earned $2,550. What did she earn each month?

_____

27. TVs were on sale for $109 each. The store took in $7,303. How many sets were sold?

_____

28. Dave worked 215 days. He earned $9,675. What did he earn each day?

_____

29. Tickets to San Jose were $35 each. The bus driver collected $1,470. How many tickets were sold?

_____

Dividing by One-Digit Numbers

You can write a division problem this way: $24 \div 6 = 4$.
Read this number sentence, "24 **divided by** 6 equals 4."

You can write the same problem another way: $6\overline{)24}$ with 4 on top
Read this number sentence, "6 **divided into** 24 equals 4."

Either way shows there are four 6's in 24.

Examples

A. Lin did the wash. He came home with 13 socks. How many pairs of socks did he have?

Write the numbers this way.

$2\overline{)13}$ How many 2's in 13?
Are there 5? Yes.
    $2 \times 5 = 10$
Are there 6? Yes.
    $2 \times 6 = 12$
Are there 7? No.
    $2 \times 7 = 14$

$\begin{array}{r} 6 \\ 2\overline{)13} \end{array}$ Write 6 in the answer.

$\begin{array}{r} 6 \\ 2\overline{)13} \\ 12 \end{array}$ Multiply. $6 \times 2 = 12$

$\begin{array}{r} 6 \\ 2\overline{)13} \\ -12 \\ \hline 1 \end{array}$ Subtract.
    $13 - 12 = 1$

$\begin{array}{r} 6 \text{ R1} \\ 2\overline{)13} \\ -12 \\ \hline 1 \end{array}$ The answer is 6 pairs of socks, with 1 sock left over. The number left over is called a **remainder. R** stands for remainder.

B. Stanley's boss pointed to a pile of oranges. "Put these in 5-pound sacks," he said. There were 47 pounds of oranges. How many sacks did Stanley fill?

Write the numbers this way.

$5\overline{)47}$ How many 5's in 47?
Are there 8? Yes.
    $5 \times 8 = 40$
Are there 9? Yes.
    $5 \times 9 = 45$
Are there 10? No.
    $5 \times 10 = 50$

$\begin{array}{r} 9 \\ 5\overline{)47} \end{array}$ Write 9 in the answer.

$\begin{array}{r} 9 \\ 5\overline{)47} \\ -45 \\ \hline 2 \end{array}$ Multiply. $9 \times 5 = 45$
Subtract. $47 - 45 = 2$

$\begin{array}{r} 9 \text{ R2} \\ 5\overline{)47} \end{array}$ The answer is 9 sacks, with 2 pounds of oranges left over.
The remainder is 2.

Write these division problems another way.

1. $81 \div 9 = 9$ $9\overline{)81}$ with 9 on top

2. $24 \div 3 = 8$ _____

3. $12 \div 4 = 3$ _____

4. $6\overline{)48}$ with 8 _____

5. $7\overline{)56}$ with 8 _____

6. $5\overline{)40}$ with 8 _____

7. $36 \div 9 = 4$ _____

8. $8\overline{)72}$ with 9 _____

9. $9\overline{)45}$ with 5 _____

10. $42 \div 7 = 6$ _____

11. $42 \div 6 = 7$ _____

12. $6\overline{)54}$ with 9 _____

Divide. Show the remainders.

13. $5\overline{)45}$

14. $4\overline{)32}$

15. $3\overline{)27}$

16. $8\overline{)34}$

17. $9\overline{)65}$

18. $7\overline{)46}$

19. $6\overline{)39}$

20. $2\overline{)11}$

21. $3\overline{)9}$

22. $8\overline{)59}$

23. $5\overline{)22}$

24. $9\overline{)53}$

Problem Solving

Solve the following problems.

25. Four people can play one game of bridge. Thirty-eight people showed up to play. How many games could be played at once? How many people could not play? ________ ________

26. During a community car wash, the community center collected \$327. If a wash was \$3 per car, how many cars were washed? ________

27. Chester is making a bookcase for his room. Each shelf will hold 18 books. If he has 72 books, how many shelves will he need? ________

28. Lil has 8 flower beds in her yard. She bought 176 tulip bulbs. How many bulbs will she plant in each flower bed? ________

29. Consuela must read a collection of 35 poems for her English class. If she has 5 days to complete this assignment, how many poems must she read each day? ________

30. The Carney family took a vacation and traveled 456 miles by car. How many miles did they drive each day, if they drove for 3 days? ________

Dividing: Two Digits in the Answer

To divide when there is more than one digit in the answer, follow
these steps until the problem is done:

Step 1   Write a digit in the answer.
Step 2   Multiply.
Step 3   Subtract.
Step 4   Bring down the next digit.

Examples

A. Jackie sold $54 worth of flowers. They
cost $2 a bunch. How many bunches
did she sell?

Divide this way.

2)54   How many 2's in 5? 2

$$\begin{array}{r} 2 \\ 2\overline{)54} \\ -4 \\ \hline 1 \end{array}$$

Write 2 above the 5.

Multiply. $2 \times 2 = 4$
Subtract. $5 - 4 = 1$

$$\begin{array}{r} 2 \\ 2\overline{)54} \\ -4\downarrow \\ \hline 14 \end{array}$$

Bring down the 4.
How many 2's in 14? 7

$$\begin{array}{r} 27 \\ 2\overline{)54} \\ -4 \\ \hline 14 \\ -14 \\ \hline 0 \end{array}$$

Write 7 above the 4.

Multiply. $7 \times 2 = 14$
Subtract. $14 - 14 = 0$

The answer is 27 bunches.

B. Srina made 50 coffee mugs. She wanted
to sell them in sets of 4. How many sets
did she have to sell?

Divide this way.

4)50   How many 4's in 5? 1

$$\begin{array}{r} 1 \\ 4\overline{)50} \\ -4 \\ \hline 1 \end{array}$$

Write 1 above the 5.

Multiply. $1 \times 4 = 4$
Subtract. $5 - 4 = 1$

$$\begin{array}{r} 1 \\ 4\overline{)50} \\ -4\downarrow \\ \hline 10 \end{array}$$

Bring down the 0.
How many 4's in 10? 2

$$\begin{array}{r} 12\ R2 \\ 4\overline{)50} \\ -4 \\ \hline 10 \\ -8 \\ \hline 2 \end{array}$$

Write 2 above the 0.

Multiply. $2 \times 4 = 8$
Subtract. $10 - 8 = 2$

The answer is 12 sets, with
2 coffee mugs left over.

Divide. Show any remainders.

1. $\begin{array}{r} 23\ \text{R}1 \\ 3\overline{)70} \\ -6 \\ \hline 10 \\ -9 \\ \hline 1 \end{array}$

2. $5\overline{)55}$

3. $3\overline{)78}$

4. $4\overline{)92}$

5. $6\overline{)84}$

6. $9\overline{)98}$

7. $7\overline{)89}$

8. $2\overline{)53}$

9. $8\overline{)95}$

Solve the following problems.

10. Jake bagged 70 pounds of onions in 4-pound sacks. How many sacks of onions did Jake bag? How many pounds were left over? _____

_____

11. Dawn sold her pictures at the art fair. She charged $6 each. She made $96. How many pictures did she sell? _____

12. Anita collected 556 cans for a recycling project. If she can put 75 cans in each bag, how many bags will she need? How many cans will be in the last bag?

_____ _____

Dividing Three-Digit and Four-Digit Numbers

To divide large numbers, follow the same steps you used to divide
two-digit numbers. You will have to repeat the steps more often.

Examples

A. Mario's pizzas cost $8 each. Friday
night Mario's made $968. How many
pizzas were sold?

$8\overline{)968}$ How many 8's in 9? 1

$\begin{array}{r} 1 \\ 8\overline{)968} \\ -8 \\ \hline 1 \end{array}$ Write 1 above the 9.
Multiply. $1 \times 8 = 8$.
Subtract. $9 - 8 = 1$

$\begin{array}{r} 12 \\ 8\overline{)968} \\ -8\downarrow \\ \hline 16 \\ -16 \\ \hline 0 \end{array}$ Bring down the 6.
How many 8's in 16? 2
   Write 2 above the 6.
Multiply. $2 \times 8 = 16$
Subtract. $16 - 16 = 0$

$\begin{array}{r} 121 \\ 8\overline{)968} \\ -8 \\ \hline 16 \\ -16\downarrow \\ \hline 08 \\ -8 \\ \hline 0 \end{array}$ Bring down the 8.
How many 8's in 8? 1
   Write 1 above the 8.
Multiply. $1 \times 8 = 8$
Subtract. $8 - 8 = 0$

There are no more numbers
to bring down.
The answer is 121 pizzas.

B. Rachel assembled 1,458 sprinklers over
16 working days. About how many
sprinklers did she assemble each day?

$16\overline{)1,458}$ How many 16's in 14?
None.
How many 16's in
145? 9

$\begin{array}{r} 9 \\ 16\overline{)1,458} \\ -1\,44 \\ \hline 1 \end{array}$ Write 9 above the 5.
Multiply. $9 \times 16 = 144$
Subtract. $145 - 144 = 1$.

$\begin{array}{r} 9 \\ 16\overline{)1,458} \\ -1\,44\downarrow \\ \hline 18 \end{array}$ Bring down the 8.
How many 16's in 18? 1

$\begin{array}{r} 91 \\ 16\overline{)1,458} \\ -1\,44 \\ \hline 18 \\ -16 \\ \hline 2 \end{array}$ Write 1 above the 8.
Multiply. $1 \times 16 = 16$
Subtract. $18 - 16 = 2$
There are no more
numbers to bring
down.

$\begin{array}{r} 91\ R2 \\ 16\overline{)1,458} \end{array}$ The answer is 91
sprinklers, with 2
extra.

Divide. Show any remainders.

1. 5)245   2. 4)244   3. 9)891   4. 70)3,290

5. 6)490   6. 8)187   7. 2)163   8. 33)2,707

9. 2)468   10. 4)956   11. 7)917   12. 25)4,825

13. 3)832   14. 6)748   15. 9)909   16. 18)2,215

Solve the following problems.

17. Keith had $345 worth of $5 bills. How many bills did he have? _____

18. Irene was packing shirts in sets of 3. She had 427 shirts. How many sets did she make? How many were left over? _____

_____

19. Robert drove 162 miles on 9 gallons of gas. How many miles did he get to the gallon? _____

Checking Division by Multiplying

In Lesson 27, you learned to check subtraction by adding. In this lesson you will learn to check division by multiplying.

Multiply your answer by the number you divided by. Make sure you add in any remainders.

Example

The Food Co-op has 1,279 pounds of ground beef for sale. The Co-op sells the beef in 3-pound packages. How many packages can be sold? Check the answer by multiplying.

```
    426 R1
3)1,279
   −12
   ‾‾‾‾
    07
    −6
   ‾‾‾‾
    19
   −18
   ‾‾‾‾
     1
```

The answer is 426 packages, with 1 pound of ground beef left over.

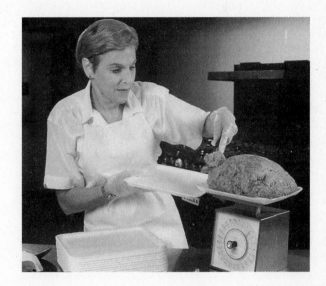

Check the answer by multiplying.

```
    4 2 6
  ×     3
  ‾‾‾‾‾‾‾
  1 , 2 7 8
+         1
  ‾‾‾‾‾‾‾
  1 , 2 7 9
```

Multiply 426 × 3.

Add the one that was left over. = the number that we divided in the first place.

426 R1 is the right answer.

Check these answers by multiplying. If the answer does not check out, find the right answer. Show your work.

1.
$$198$$
$$4\overline{)793}$$

$$198$$
$$\times\ \ 4$$
$$\overline{792}$$
Wrong.

$$198\ R1$$
$$4\overline{)793}$$
$$-4$$
$$\overline{\ \ 39}$$
$$-36$$
$$\overline{\ \ \ 33}$$
$$-32$$
$$\overline{\ \ \ \ \ 1}$$

2.
$$146$$
$$3\overline{)438}$$

3.
$$321\ R6$$
$$6\overline{)1,927}$$

4.
$$1,227\ R3$$
$$7\overline{)8,592}$$

5.
$$1,158$$
$$8\overline{)9,256}$$

6.
$$1,116\ R8$$
$$9\overline{)1,052}$$

7.
$$853\ R3$$
$$5\overline{)9,268}$$

8.
$$1,184\ R1$$
$$8\overline{)8,473}$$

9.
$$812\ R2$$
$$6\overline{)4,873}$$

10.
$$1,432\ R1$$
$$3\overline{)4,296}$$

11. $\dfrac{1,571 \text{ R}3}{4)6,287}$

12. $\dfrac{147}{7)1,028}$

13. $\dfrac{349}{8)2,792}$

14. $\dfrac{1,421 \text{ R}1}{6)8,526}$

15. $\dfrac{962 \text{ R}1}{4)3,849}$

16. $\dfrac{3,818}{2)7,638}$

Problem Solving

Solve the following problems. Check each answer by multiplying.

17. Beth bought a used car for $2,586. She paid for it in six months. She paid the same amount every month. How much did she pay each month? _____

18. Rick has saved $5 a week since he started working. He has $1,055 in the bank. How many weeks has he been working? _____

19. Yoko was packing books 6 to a box. There were 1,399 books. How many full boxes did she pack? _____

Finding College Costs

At City College it takes a total of 60 credits to graduate. Each class is worth 2 or more credits. The school charges by the credit. There is one rate for city students. There is a different rate for out-of-state students. There is a third rate for foreign students. The college also charges other fees.

Here is what it costs to go to City College.

Fees	City Students	Out-of-State Students	Foreign Students
Sign-up fee	$25 each term	$50 each term	$ 75 each term
Classes—			
per credit	45	90	100
Student fee	25	30	35
Health service—			
students taking			
up to 5 credits	35	70	100
students taking			
6 credits or more	50	75	80

Using the information about students fees, answer these questions.

1. A city student wants to take 6 credits. What is the cost? _____

2. How much are the other fees for a city student? _____

3. How much will going to school cost in all for a city student? _____

4. A student who lives in another state needs 30 more credits to graduate. How much will the classes cost? _____

5. If a student takes 12 credits each term, how many terms will it take to get 60 credits in all? _____

6. A foreign student took English classes worth 6 credits and a business class for 5 credits. How much did his classes cost? _____

Dividing by Two-Digit Numbers

When dividing by two-digit numbers, follow the steps you have been using for other division problems. However, the extra digit might be confusing. You may have to try more than one number in the answer before you reach the one that is not too large or too small.

Example

A landscaper has 13 lots to landscape. She has 67 shrubs. She wants to use the same number of shrubs on each lot. How many shrubs can she use on each lot?

$13\overline{)67}$ How many 1's in 6? 6

$$\begin{array}{r} 6 \\ 13\overline{)67} \\ -78 \end{array}$$
Try 6 in the answer. Write it over the 7.
Multiply. $6 \times 13 = 78$
Subtract. 78 is too big to subtract.
6 is too big in the answer.

$$\begin{array}{r} 5\ R2 \\ 13\overline{)67} \\ -65 \\ \hline 2 \end{array}$$
Try 5 in the answer.
Multiply. $5 \times 13 = 65$
Subtract. $67 - 65 = 2$

The landscaper can use 5 shrubs on each lot. She will have 2 left over.

Practice

Divide. Show any remainders.

1. $32\overline{)96}$ 2. $14\overline{)84}$ 3. $23\overline{)92}$ 4. $18\overline{)54}$

5. $17\overline{)97}$ 6. $27\overline{)86}$ 7. $35\overline{)94}$ 8. $24\overline{)87}$

9. $32\overline{)85}$ 10. $27\overline{)95}$ 11. $33\overline{)97}$ 12. $13\overline{)76}$

13. $12\overline{)94}$ 14. $13\overline{)84}$ 15. $31\overline{)67}$ 16. $16\overline{)96}$

17. $25\overline{)96}$ 18. $28\overline{)88}$ 19. $15\overline{)92}$ 20. $28\overline{)99}$

Problem Solving

Solve the following problems.

21. Twenty-eight people paid $84 to ride a bus. How much was each ticket? _____

22. There were 24 people at the picnic. There were 75 pieces of chicken. If the chicken pieces are divided equally, how many pieces could each person have? How many pieces would be left over? _____   _____

23. Buzz drove 88 miles on 11 gallons of gas. How many miles to the gallon did he get? _____

24. Nadim had 97 pounds of rock salt. He put it in 15-pound bags. How many bags did he fill? How many pounds of salt were left over? _____   _____

154

Setting Savings Goals

Some people make a plan for saving money. They save the same amount every week or month to reach a goal.

Diane joined the Vacation Club. She will save $15 a week. She wants to go on vacation in 25 weeks. How much money will she have?

```
      2 5      number of weeks
  ×     1 5    weekly goal
  $ 3 7 5      total savings
```

Carmen has a 12-week summer job. She needs $1272 to pay for school in the fall. If she is paid each week, how much must she save each week? If she is paid only once a month and she works for three months, how much must she save each month?

A. number of weeks 12

```
      $106      weekly goal
  12)$1272      total needed
```

B. number of months 3

```
      $424      monthly goal
  3)$1272       total needed
```

Set a savings goal. Decide how much you have to save each week to reach it.

Find these weekly, monthly, and total savings goals.

1. Norm brings his own lunch to work. By doing this, he can save $10 a week. How much will he save in a year? (Norm works 50 weeks in a year.)

   _____

2. Jimm saves $12 a week for a compact disc player. The player costs $360. How long will it take to save the money?

   _____

3. Mr. Swanson made out his tax form. He found he will owe $126. How much must he save in 4 months to pay for his taxes?

   _____

4. The Santiagos want to buy some land. The down payment is $1,500. They want to buy the land a year from now. What is their monthly savings goal?

   _____

5. Sam got a raise of an extra $14 a week. If he saves that amount, how much will he have in 30 weeks?

   _____

Estimating Answers

Estimation is very useful in division. If you round your numbers before you divide, it is easier to find how many times the one number will go into the other.

Example

The City Playhouse sold 639 tickets for the Friday night performance. The ushers were told to fill each row. There are 36 seats in a row. How many rows will be filled? How many people will sit in the last row?

To estimate an answer:

$36\overline{)639}$ Round 36 to the nearest ten—40.
$40 \times 10 = 400$, less than 639.
$40 \times 20 = 800$, more than 639.
The answer is between 10 and 20.

> **MATH HINT**
>
> It helps to estimate answers first when working with larger numbers. Then you can find the exact answer more quickly.

To find the exact answer:

$36\overline{)639}$ How many 3's in 6? 2
   But we already know the answer is between 10 and 20.
   The first number in the answer must be 1.

$\dfrac{1}{36\overline{)639}}$

$\begin{array}{r} 1 \\ 36\overline{)639} \\ -36 \\ \hline 27 \end{array}$ Write 1 above the 3.

   Multiply. $1 \times 36 = 36$
   Subtract. $63 - 36 = 27$

$\begin{array}{r} 1 \\ 36\overline{)639} \\ -36\downarrow \\ \hline 279 \end{array}$ Bring down the 9.
   How many 3's in 27? 9
   Estimate to see if 9 will work.
   $9 \times 40 = 360$. Too big. Try 8.
   $8 \times 40 = 320$. Also too big.

```
  17 R27    Try 7 in the answer.
36)639      Write 7 above the 9.
 −36
  279
 −252       Multiply. 7 × 36 = 252
   27       Subtract. 279 − 252 = 27
            There are no more numbers to bring down.

            The ushers filled 17 rows.
            The last row had 27 people.
```

Practice

Estimate the answers. Then find the exact answers.

```
        19 R11
1.  28)543        30 × 10 = 300        2.  32)786          Between
    −28           30 × 20 = 600
    263
   −252           Between                                  _____ and _____
     11
                  __10__ and __20__
```

```
3.  43)943        Between              4.  71)859          Between


                  _____ and _____                          _____ and _____
```

```
5.  83)965        Between              6.  51)650          Between


                  _____ and _____                          _____ and _____
```

```
7.  68)879        Between              8.  49)587          Between


                  _____ and _____                          _____ and _____
```

```
9.  34)720        Between              10. 67)740          Between


                  _____ and _____                          _____ and _____
```

157

11.
$$\begin{array}{r} 133 \text{ R4} \\ 36\overline{)4{,}792} \\ -3\,6 \quad\;\; \\ \hline 1\;19 \quad \\ -1\,08 \quad \\ \hline 112 \\ -108 \\ \hline 4 \end{array}$$

Between   _100_ and _200_

12. $23\overline{)2{,}903}$ Between   _____ and _____

13. $43\overline{)3{,}562}$ Between   _____ and _____

14. $89\overline{)6{,}362}$ Between   _____ and _____

Problem Solving

Solve the following problems.

15. Margo printed 378 note cards. She sold them in boxes of 12. How many boxes did she have for sale? How many cards remain?

_____   _____

16. Arturo's Bakery made 6,048 dinner rolls. They were wrapped 24 to a box. How many boxes were there?

_____

Dividing by Three-Digit Numbers

To divide by three-digit numbers, use estimation. Look at the first digit or digits of the divisor and try to determine "about" how many times that number will divide into the number to be divided (dividend).

Examples

A. A freight car carried 815 sacks of coffee. Dock workers loaded the sacks onto carts. Each cart could hold 294 sacks. How many full carts were there? How many sacks were on the last cart?

$294\overline{)815}$

Estimation:
Round 294 to 300.
How many 300's in 815?
$300 \times 2 = 600$
$300 \times 3 = 900$
The answer is between **2** and **3**.

$$294\overline{)815} \quad \begin{array}{r} 2 \\ \hline \end{array}$$
$$-588$$
$$\overline{227}$$

Try 2 in the answer.
There were 2 full carts.
The last cart had 227 sacks of coffee.

B. 9,684 school children in the South District needed shots. The nurses could handle 367 children a day. How many full days did the nurses have to work? How many children got shots on the final day?

$367\overline{)9,684}$

Estimation:
Round 367 to 400.
How many 400's in 9,684?
$400 \times 20 = 8000$
$400 \times 30 = 12,000$
The answer is between **20** and **30**.

How many 400's in 9? 0
How many 400's in 96? 0
How many 400's in 968? 2

$$\begin{array}{r} 2 \\ 367\overline{)9,684} \\ -7\ 34 \\ \hline 2\ 34 \end{array}$$

Write 2 above the 8.

Multiply.

Subtract.

$$\begin{array}{r} 2 \\ 367\overline{)9,684} \\ -7\ 34\downarrow \\ \hline 2,344 \end{array}$$

Bring down the 4.
How many 400's in 2,344?
$400 \times 5 = 2000$
$400 \times 6 = 2400$

$$\begin{array}{r} 25 \\ 367\overline{)9,684} \\ -6\ 34 \\ \hline 2,344 \\ -1,835 \\ \hline 509 \end{array}$$

Try 5 in the answer.

$509 > 367$.

5 in the answer is too small.

Estimating does not always work.

```
          26        Try 6 in the answer.
367)9,684
     −7 34
      2,344         The nurses had to work 26 full days.
     −2,202         142 children got shots the final day.
        142
```

--- **Practice** ---

Divide. Show any remainders.

```
           8
1. 397)3,176        2. 614)3,070        3. 779)7,011
    −3,176
         0
```

```
4. 558)3,362        5. 212)1,498        6. 784)6,295
```

```
7. 296)7,992        8. 821)19,704       9. 473)29,314
```

--- **Problem Solving** ---

Solve the following problems.

10. The author of *Reading and Writing English* sold 756 copies. Her sales total was $18,900. What was the cost of each copy?

11. An author sold books in a three-state area. On one trip the author covered 1,100 miles—traveling 220 miles a day. How many days did the author travel?

LIFE SKILL

Fringe Benefits

Companies pay their workers in two ways. The first is money. The second is called **fringe benefits.** These fringe benefits are worth money and are part of total pay. Some of these benefits could be low cost meals, days off, or health insurance.

Here are the facts about two jobs.

Job A

Base pay	$15,925
Paid holidays	10
Paid personal or sick days	10
Work week	36 hours
Insurance plan	no
Company bus	yes

Job B

Base pay	$14,994
Paid holidays	12
Paid personal or sick days	15
Work week	36 hours
Insurance plan	yes
Company bus	no

1. What is the difference in base pay between the two jobs? _____

2. Job A has 245 working days a year. What does it pay per day? _____

3. Job B has 238 working days a year. What does it pay per day? _____

4. If public transportation costs $2 a day to get to and from either job, what is Job A's company bus worth? _____

5. It would cost $32 a month for the kind of insurance Job B offers. What is Job B's insurance worth per year? _____

6. Let's say that both jobs are about the same in other ways. Which job would you take? Why? _____

Dividing With Zeros in the Answer

Remember these steps for division:

Step 1   Write a digit in the answer.

Step 2   Multiply.

Step 3   Subtract.

Step 4   Bring down the next digit.

Example

$$\begin{array}{r} 8 \\ 8\overline{)6{,}459} \\ -6\,4 \\ \hline 05 \end{array}$$

How many 8's in 64? 8
Multiply. $8 \times 8 = 64$
Subtract. $64 - 64 = 0$
Bring down the 5.

$$\begin{array}{r} 80 \\ 8\overline{)6{,}459} \\ -6\,4 \\ \hline 05 \\ -\ 0 \\ \hline 59 \end{array}$$

How many 8's in 5? 0
Write 0 above the 5.

Multiply. $0 \times 8 = 0$
Subtract. $5 - 0 = 5$
Bring down the 9.

$$\begin{array}{r} 80 \\ 8\overline{)6{,}459} \\ -6\,4 \\ \hline 059 \end{array}$$

A **shorter way** is to write 0 above the 5 and bring down the 9, without multiplying by the 0.

$$\begin{array}{r} 807\ \text{R3} \\ 8\overline{)6{,}459} \\ -6\,4 \\ \hline 059 \\ -56 \\ \hline 3 \end{array}$$

How many 8's in 59? 7
Write 7 above the 9.

Multiply. $7 \times 8 = 56$
Subtract. $59 - 56 = 3$
No more numbers to bring down.

The answer is 807 R3.

> **MATH HINT**
>
> **U**se these steps for all digits, including zeros.

Divide. Show any remainders.

1.
```
      504
  7)3,528
   -3 5
      028
      -28
        0
```

2. 6)1,854

3. 9)6,345

4. 63)2,520

5. 26)2,087

6. 38)2,666

7. 46)2,311

8. 62)4,968

9. 59)1,777

10. 5)3,542

11. 8)4,850

12. 4)2,806

13. 155)46,810

14. 217)23,005

15. 246)100,624

LIFE SKILL

Finding Average Expenses for a Budget

The Morenos want to make a budget. They know their **fixed monthly expenses,** such as rent and car payments. They need to know how much to budget for **variable expenses**—expenses that differ each month. They decide to keep a record of what they spend monthly for three months, then find the **average monthly expense** for each item. Help them complete their notebook below.

To find a monthly average, find the total of the monthly expenses. Then divide by the number of months.

	Month 1	Month 2	Month 3	3-month total	average
Food	$143	$136	$147	1. $426	2. $142
Car: Gas and repairs	$77	$36	$45	3. ___	4. ___
Telephone	$36	$48	$54	5. ___	6. ___
Entertainment	$63.	$48	$51	7. ___	8. ___
Clothes	$150	$180	$144	9. ___	10. ___
Gifts	$15	$24	$21	11. ___	12. ___
Health care	$96	$28	$35	13. ___	14. ___
Other	$63	$78	$81	15. ___	16. ___

Problem Solving—Key Words to Choose the Operation

When solving problems, look for the key words to help you determine the operation or operations you must perform. The following steps will also help you.

Step 1 Read the problem and underline the key words. These words will relate to some mathematics computation.

Step 2 Make a plan to solve the problem. Ask yourself, Should I add, subtract, multiply, divide, round, or compare? You may have to do more than one operation for the same problem. You may also be able to estimate your answer.

Step 3 Find the solution.

Step 4 Check the answer. Ask yourself, Is the answer reasonable? Did you find what you were asked for?

Remember these key words:

Addition	Subtraction	Multiplication	Division
altogether	decreased by	product	quotient
both	difference	how much	per
increase	remainder	of	for each
sum	diminished by	apiece	average
total	how much less	multiplied by	shared
together	how much more		
in all			

Example

The table shows sales from July through December.
Use the table and the list of key words to help you answer the questions that follow.

July	$34,679
August	$39,804
September	$41,925
October	$38,152
November	$40,009
December	$41,290

What is the difference in the sales figures for December and July?

Step 1 Determine the difference in sales figures. The key word is **difference.**

Step 2 The key word indicates subtraction.

Step 3 Find the solution.

$$\begin{array}{r} \$\,4\,1\,,\,2\,9\,0 \quad \text{Dec. Sales} \\ -\ \ 3\,4\,,\,6\,7\,9 \quad \text{July Sales} \\ \hline \$\ \ \ 6\,,\,6\,1\,1 \end{array}$$

Step 4 Check the answer. If you add $6,611 to $34,679, you will get $41,290. The answer is correct.

Practice

Continue to use the table on sales to answer Questions 1–4. Circle the key words that helped you choose the operation.

1. How much were the total sales for October, November, and December?

2. There were five people selling in December. If each sold the same amount, how much did each one sell?

3. If the company had a year of monthly sales equal to the July sales, what would the total be?

4. How much were the total sales for July through December?

5. Juana worked 215 days last year. She made $9,675 in all. How much did she make each day?

6. Five workers made $6 an hour for 8 hours. How much did they make altogether?

7. Amina works in a day-care center. There are 35 children in her room in the morning. There are 42 in the afternoon. How many children does she care for altogether?

8. Irwin had 54 shirts to iron at work. By lunchtime, he had ironed 16. How many shirts remained to be ironed?

9. Nori drove 192 miles. She used 12 gallons of gas. How many miles did she get per gallon?

Posttest

Divide. Show any remainders.

1. $6\overline{)42}$ **2.** $8\overline{)2,590}$ **3.** $3\overline{)584}$

4. $5\overline{)47}$ **5.** $3\overline{)398}$ **6.** $8\overline{)4,335}$

7. $24\overline{)86}$ **8.** $37\overline{)8,650}$ **9.** $13\overline{)6,355}$

10. $26\overline{)87}$ **11.** $67\overline{)28,888}$ **12.** $34\overline{)7,422}$

13. $132\overline{)15,050}$ **14.** $103\overline{)5,560}$ **15.** $294\overline{)30,282}$

16. $148\overline{)3,848}$ **17.** $217\overline{)71,827}$ **18.** $387\overline{)132,349}$

Estimate the answers.

19. $59\overline{)1,070}$ Between _____ and _____   **20.** $22\overline{)1,190}$ Between _____ and _____

21. $17\overline{)3,662}$ Between _____ and _____   **22.** $21\overline{)5,380}$ Between _____ and _____

Find the answers. Check by multiplying.

23. $32\overline{)84}$ **24.** $49\overline{)787}$ **25.** $85\overline{)1,701}$

26. $302\overline{)9,362}$ **27.** $489\overline{)49,390}$ **28.** $113\overline{)26,668}$

Problem Solving

Solve the following problems.

29. Tilman drove 192 miles. He used 12 gallons of gas. How many miles did he get per gallon?   _____

30. Mia worked 32 days. She made $1376. How much money did she make each day?   _____

31. Jeff drove a truck the same distance each day. He was on the road for 15 days. He covered 6,135 miles. How many miles did he drive per day?   _____

32. Mrs. Gomez worked 236 days last year. She made $11,800. How much did she make each day?   _____

33. Gordon's car cost $6,950. The first year he owned it, he paid $425 for insurance, $118 for tuneups, and $189 for repairs. Gas and oil cost $668. What was the total cost of the car?   _____

Using Whole Number Skills

Write using exponents.

1. $4 \times 4 \times 4$ _____

2. $5 \times 5 \times 5 \times 5 \times 5 \times 5$ _____

3. 8×8 _____

4. $2 \times 2 \times 2 \times 2$ _____

Evaluate.

5. 5^2 _____

6. 3^3 _____

7. 10^4 _____

8. 9^2 _____

Evaluate using the order of operations.

9. $2 + 16 - 4 \times 2$ _____

10. $3^2 - 6 \times 1 + 5$ _____

11. $(4 + 8) \times 2 + 2$ _____

12. $24 \div 4 \times 2 + 3$ _____

13. $(4 + 5) \times (5 \times 2)$ _____

14. $3 \times 2^3 - 7$ _____

Solve the following equations. Check your work.

15. $x + 6 = 12$ _____

16. $x - 8 = 19$ _____

17. $y + 24 = 45$ _____

18. $4a = 24$ _____

19. $\frac{n}{4} = 3$ _____

20. $20 = x - 5$ _____

21. $15 = z + 15$ _____

22. $5 = \frac{t}{2}$ _____

23. $9v = 36$ _____

24. $16 = r - 9$ _____

25. $\frac{m}{3} = 6$ _____

26. $63 = 7j$ _____

27. $26 = p + 7$ _____

28. $r - 18 = 21$ _____

29. $8b = 64$ _____

30. $\frac{n}{5} = 10$ _____

Problem Solving

**Write an equation and use it to solve the following problems.
Let x = the unknown.**

31. Joe wants to buy a new printer for his computer. Printers are on sale for $209. The regular price is $250. How much is the savings?

32. A new bicycle retails for $399. This week the bike store is offering a $30 off coupon in the newspaper. How much would the bicycle cost with the coupon?

_____ _____   _____ _____

Exponents

A raised smaller number to the right of a number is an **exponent.** Exponents are used to represent *repeated* multiplication. The number multiplied times itself is called the **base.**

Examples

A. Write $3 \times 3 \times 3 \times 3 \times 3$ using exponents.

The first thing you must do is count how many 3's are being repeated. In this problem there are 5. Therefore, 5 would be your exponent and the answer is written like this:

$3 \times 3 \times 3 \times 3 \times 3 = 3^5$

B. Evaluate 6^3

$6 \times 6 \times 6 = 216$

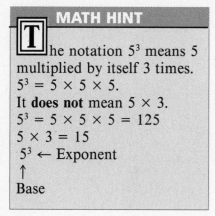

MATH HINT

The notation 5^3 means 5 multiplied by itself 3 times.
$5^3 = 5 \times 5 \times 5$.
It **does not** mean 5×3.
$5^3 = 5 \times 5 \times 5 = 125$
$5 \times 3 = 15$
$5^3 \leftarrow$ Exponent
$\uparrow$
Base

Write using exponents.

1. 5×5 _____

2. $7 \times 7 \times 7 \times 7$ _____

3. $3 \times 3 \times 3$ _____

4. 10×10 _____

5. $1 \times 1 \times 1 \times 1 \times 1 \times 1$ _____

6. $6 \times 6 \times 6 \times 6 \times 6 \times 6$ _____

7. $2 \times 2 \times 2 \times 2 \times 2$ _____

8. $0 \times 0 \times 0 \times 0$ _____

9. $4 \times 4 \times 4$ _____

10. $8 \times 8 \times 8 \times 8 \times 8$ _____

Evaluate.

11. 2^5 _____

12. 4^2 _____

13. 3^3 _____

14. 7^2 _____

15. 5^4 _____

16. 8^2 _____

17. 1^5 _____

18. 10^3 _____

19. 2^3 _____

20. 4^2 _____

Order of Operations

Sometimes you will have to solve problems that have a mixture of many operations, including addition, subtraction, multiplication, and division. To do this, you should follow the order of operations shown below:

Step 1 Calculate everything inside parentheses.

Step 2 Simplify all exponents.

Step 3 Calculate multiplication or division operations, moving from left to right.

Step 4 Calculate addition or subtraction operations, moving from left to right.

Symbols you should know:

Addition	+	$3 + 4 = 7$
Subtraction	–	$4 - 3 = 1$
Multiplication	×	$3 \times 4 = 12$
	•	$3 \cdot 4 = 12$
	( )	$3(4) = 12$
Division	÷	$12 \div 4 = 3$
	—	$\frac{12}{4} = 3$

> **MATH HINT**
>
> **A**n easy way to remember the order of operations is by the following phrase.
> PLEASE — P stands for **Parentheses**. Do operations in parentheses *first*.
> EXCUSE — E stands for **Exponents**. Do all of these after any parentheses.
> MY — M stands for **Multiplication**.
> DEAR — D stands for **Division**.
> AUNT — A stands for **Addition**.
> SALLY — S stands for **Subtraction**.

Examples

A. $3 + (6 \times 2) = ?$

Step 1 $6 \times 2 = 12$

Step 2 No exponents to simplify

Step 3 No multiplication or division to calculate

Step 4 $3 + 12 = 15$

B. $5 + 2 \times 4^2 = ?$

Step 1 No calculations inside parentheses.

Step 2 $4^2 = 4 \times 4 = 16$

Step 3 $2 \times 16 = 32$

Step 4 $5 + 32 = 37$

C. $2 + 4 \times 6 \div 2 = ?$

Since there are no parentheses or exponents in this example, you should move to Step 3.

Step 3 $4 \times 6 = 24$
$$\downarrow$$
$$2 + 24 \div 2 = ?$$
$$24 \div 2 = 12$$
$$\downarrow$$
$$2 + 12 = ?$$

Calculate multiplication

and then

division operations.

Step 4 $2 + 12 = 14$

Practice

Which operation would you perform first?

1. $24 - 6 \div 2 \times 9 + 6^2$ _____

2. $3 \times 4 + (4 + 7) \times 2$ _____

3. $16 \div (10 - 8) \times 5$ _____

4. $5 - 2 \times 4 \div 4$ _____

5. $6 + 5 - 3 + 10$ _____

Evaluate.

6. $4 \times 5 + 3 =$ _____

7. $10 - 5 + 2^3 =$ _____

8. $6 \times (3 + 2) =$ _____

9. $10 \times 2 \div 5 =$ _____

10. $9 + 6 \div 3 =$ _____

11. $15 - 2 + 6 - 9 =$ _____

12. $2 + 6 \div 2 \times 4 =$ _____

13. $3^2 \times 4 - 2 =$ _____

14. $(6 - 1) + (5 + 2) =$ _____

15. $40 - (5 \times 5) + 10 =$ _____

16. $9 + 27 \div 9 =$ _____

17. $9 + 12 \div 3 \times 2 =$ _____

18. $4 + (3 \times 5) - 2 =$ _____

19. $100 \div 10 + 10 =$ _____

20. $3 \times (2 + 4) - 15 =$ _____

21. $20 \div 5 + 5 \times 3 =$ _____

22. $3 + 4^2 - 8 =$ _____

23. $(25 \times 2) \div 10 + 5 =$ _____

24. $6 \times (4 + 5) - 40 =$ _____

25. $8 - 3 \times 2 + 4 \times 6 =$ _____

Equations and Solutions

An **equation** is a statement in which two quantities are equal.

$x + 4 = 10$ means that 10 is equal to some number plus 4.

The missing number is called an **unknown** which can be represented by the variable x. The value for x that makes the equation true is the **solution**. In the equation, $x + 4 = 10$, 6 is the solution.

Examples

A. Is 13 a solution for $x - 4 = 9$?
$13 - 4 = 9$
This is true, so 13 is a solution.

B. Is 15 a solution for $x - 4 = 9$?
$15 - 4 \neq 9$
This is not true, so 15 is not a solution.

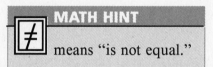

MATH HINT
$\neq$ means "is not equal."

Practice

For each equation, circle the correct solution.

1. $x + 5 = 15$	5	10	15
2. $x - 6 = 9$	15	3	12
3. $x + 3 = 29$	31	25	26
4. $x - 10 = 20$	10	20	30
5. $2 + x = 12$	4	6	10
6. $5 + x = 12$	15	7	4
7. $x + 14 = 32$	28	18	20
8. $x - 14 = 14$	14	10	28

Addition Equations

To find the solution to an addition equation, you must **subtract.** Any operation performed on one side of the equation must also be performed on the other.

Examples

A. This is an addition problem.

Solve $x + 5 = 16$

$$x + 5 = 16$$
$$\underline{-5 \quad -5}$$

Subtract 5 from each side of the equation.

$$x + 0 = 11$$
$$x = 11$$

B. This is an addition problem.

Solve $22 = x + 3$

It does not matter which side x is on. You still solve the problem the same way you solved in Example A.

$$22 = x + 3$$
$$\underline{-3 \qquad -3}$$

Subtract 3 from each side of the equation.

$$19 = x + 0$$
$$19 = x$$

Practice

Solve these equations. Check your answers.

1. $x + 3 = 17$ _____

2. $x + 20 = 30$ _____

3. $x + 11 = 15$ _____

4. $x + 9 = 32$ _____

5. $x + 5 = 25$ _____

6. $x + 7 = 18$ _____

7. $15 = x + 7$ _____

8. $30 = x + 9$ _____

9. $x + 12 = 17$ _____

10. $21 = x + 5$ _____

11. $19 = x + 6$ _____

12. $x + 15 = 38$ _____

13. $19 = x + 9$ _____

14. $45 = x + 20$ _____

15. $80 = x + 50$ _____

16. $x + 26 = 52$ _____

Subtraction Equations

To find the solution to a subtraction equation, you must **add.** Any operation performed on one side of the equation must also be performed on the other.

A. This is a subtraction problem.

Solve $x - 5 = 12$.

$$x - 5 = 12$$
$$\underline{+5 \quad +5}$$ Add 5 to each side of the equation.

$$x + 0 = 17$$
$$x = 17$$

B. This is a subtraction problem.

Solve $22 = x - 8$

It does not matter which side x is on. You still solve the problem the same way you solved Example A.

$$22 = x - 8$$
$$\underline{+8 \qquad +8}$$ Add 8 to each side of the equation.
$$30 = x + 0$$
$$30 = x$$

Solve these equations. Check your answers.

1. $x - 6 = 17$ _____

2. $x - 5 = 3$ _____

3. $x - 11 = 11$ _____

4. $x - 9 = 12$ _____

5. $x - 5 = 5$ _____

6. $x - 7 = 28$ _____

7. $25 = x - 7$ _____

8. $3 = x - 9$ _____

9. $x - 12 = 17$ _____

10. $21 = x - 10$ _____

11. $19 = x - 9$ _____

12. $x - 4 = 18$ _____

13. $15 = x - 9$ _____

14. $4 = x - 20$ _____

15. $80 = x - 10$ _____

16. $x - 26 = 22$ _____

17. $x - 25 = 50$ _____

18. $36 = x - 9$ _____

Multiplication Equations

The rules that applied to equations that have only addition and subtraction can be applied to multiplication.

To find a solution to a multiplication equation, you must **divide.** Any operation performed on one side of the equation must also be performed on the other.

Examples

A. Solve $5b = 45$

$5b = 45$ $5b$ means b multiplied by 5

$$\frac{5b}{5} = \frac{45}{5}$$

$$\frac{\overset{1}{\cancel{5}}b}{\underset{1}{\cancel{5}}} = \frac{\overset{9}{\cancel{45}}}{\underset{1}{\cancel{5}}}$$

To solve this problem you must divide both sides by 5.

$b = 9$

B. Solve $32 = 8x$

$$\frac{32}{8} = \frac{8x}{8}$$

To solve this problem you must divide both sides by 8.

$$\frac{\overset{4}{\cancel{32}}}{\underset{1}{\cancel{8}}} = \frac{\overset{1}{\cancel{8}}x}{\underset{1}{\cancel{8}}}$$

$4 = x$

MATH HINT

When a number and a variable (letter) are written next to each other, you must multiply. You don't need to use a multiplication sign when working with variables.

Practice

Solve these equations. Check your answers.

1. $7x = 35$ _____

2. $6x = 18$ _____

3. $8a = 8$ _____

4. $3y = 21$ _____

5. $4p = 32$ _____

6. $5x = 30$ _____

7. $48 = 6a$ _____

8. $55 = 11x$ _____

9. $9x = 72$ _____

10. $100 = 20d$ _____

11. $39 = 13f$ _____

12. $5x = 5$ _____

13. $9x = 54$ _____

14. $16 = 2x$ _____

Division Equations

The rules that applied to equations that have only addition and subtraction can be applied to division.

To find a solution to a division equation, you must **multiply.** Any operation performed on one side of the equation must also be performed on the other.

Examples

A. Solve $9 = \frac{m}{3}$

$\frac{m}{3}$ means m divided by 3

$3 \cdot 9 = \frac{m}{3} \cdot 3$ The opposite operation is multiplication. Multiply both sides by 3 to solve.

$3 \cdot 9 = \frac{m}{\cancel{3}} \cdot \cancel{3}^{1}$ Multiply by 3.

$27 = m$

B. Solve $\frac{x}{5} = 10$

$5 \cdot \frac{x}{5} = 10 \cdot 5$ You must multiply both sides by 5 to solve.

$\cancel{5}^{1} \cdot \frac{x}{\cancel{5}_{1}} = 10 \cdot 5$

$x = 50$ Multiply by 5.

Practice

Solve these equations. Check your answers.

1. $\frac{b}{8} = 3$ _____

2. $\frac{x}{5} = 5$ _____

3. $6 = \frac{a}{2}$ _____

4. $\frac{d}{4} = 9$ _____

5. $15 = \frac{f}{3}$ _____

6. $\frac{n}{7} = 9$ _____

7. $11 = \frac{m}{11}$ _____

8. $10 = \frac{n}{6}$ _____

9. $\frac{c}{12} = 4$ _____

10. $25 = \frac{x}{4}$ _____

11. $\frac{y}{7} = 7$ _____

12. $9 = \frac{c}{10}$ _____

13. $\frac{x}{4} = 8$ _____

14. $16 = \frac{y}{2}$ _____

Problem Solving—Using Equations

Throughout this book, you have been doing problem-solving lessons. Review the following steps.

Step 1 Read the problem and underline the key words. These words will usually relate to some mathematics reasoning computation.

Step 2 Make a plan to solve the problem. Ask yourself, Should I add, subtract, multiply, divide, round, or compare? You may have to do more than one operation for the same problem.

Step 3 Find the solution. Use your math knowledge to find your answer.

Step 4 Check the answer. Ask yourself, Is the answer reasonable? Did you find what you were asked for?

The third step is to find the solution by using your math knowledge. The use of equations can help you find the solution.

Example

A t-shirt costs $14. On sale it is $9. How much is the savings?

After reading the problem and looking for any key words, you know you will be determining the savings. It should be understood that the sale price is less than the regular price.

To find the solution, you can use equations.

Let $x =$ the amount of the savings.

Sample Equations:
$$14 - 9 = x \quad \text{or} \quad x + 9 = 14$$
$$5 = x \qquad\qquad \underline{-9 = -9}$$
$$x + 0 = 5$$
$$x = 5$$

Step 4 Check the answer.
$$14 - 9 = 5 \quad \text{or} \quad 5 + 9 = 14$$
$$5 = 5 \qquad\qquad 14 = 14$$

Write an equation and use it to solve the following problems.
Let x = the unknown amount.

1. A pack of tube socks normally costs $8. It is on sale this week for $5. What is the savings?

2. The savings on a new dress is $12. The regular price for the dress is $80. What is the sale price?

_____ _____

_____ _____

3. A big screen TV is on sale for $1200. The TV is normally priced at $1550. How much is the savings?

4. A new car is listed for $12,995. There is a $1500 rebate with the car. How much is the car after the rebate?

_____ _____

_____ _____

5. A sofa and chair are on sale for $650. This is a savings of $125. How much do they cost normally?

6. In a new housing development, a large lot is $30,000. A smaller lot can be purchased for $24,600. How much would you save by buying the smaller lot?

_____ _____

_____ _____

Posttest

Write using exponents.

1. 5×5 _____

2. $2 \times 2 \times 2$ _____

3. $9 \times 9 \times 9$ _____

4. $7 \times 7 \times 7 \times 7 \times 7$ _____

Evaluate.

5. 6^2 _____

6. 2^3 _____

7. 3^4 _____

8. 8^2 _____

Evaluate using the order of operations.

9. $3 + 26 - 5 \times 2$ _____

10. $5^2 - 8 \times 2 + 4$ _____

11. $(3 + 7) \times 3 + 3$ _____

12. $28 \div 4 \times 3 + 9$ _____

13. $(5 + 15) \times (2 \times 2)$ _____

14. $2 \times 3^3 - 8$ _____

Solve the following equations. Check your work.

15. $x + 8 = 22$ _____

16. $x - 9 = 29$ _____

17. $y + 4 = 15$ _____

18. $6a = 24$ _____

19. $\frac{p}{5} = 3$ _____

20. $21 = x - 7$ _____

21. $25 = z + 5$ _____

22. $4 = \frac{t}{8}$ _____

23. $8v = 48$ _____

24. $14 = r - 8$ _____

25. $\frac{m}{6} = 7$ _____

26. $72 = 9j$ _____

27. $35 = p + 7$ _____

28. $r - 28 = 11$ _____

29. $5b = 45$ _____

30. $\frac{n}{9} = 18$ _____

Write an equation and use it to solve the following problems.
Let x = the unknown amount.

31. Al wants to buy a new lawnmower. They are on sale for $399. The regular price is $450. How much is the savings?

32. A new house normally costs $110,000. During the month of February the builder is offering a $5000 off special. How much would this house cost with the February special?

_____   _____

Multiplication and Division Posttest

Complete these number sentences.

1. $5 \times 6 =$ _____

2. _____ $\div 9 = 45$

3. $8 \times$ _____ $= 48$

4. $21 \div$ _____ $= 7$

Write four different number sentences using 7, 9, and 63.

5. _____   _____   _____   _____

Multiply.

6. $\begin{array}{r} 57 \\ \times\ 7 \\ \hline \end{array}$

7. $\begin{array}{r} 76 \\ \times\ 3 \\ \hline \end{array}$

8. $\begin{array}{r} 42 \\ \times\ 4 \\ \hline \end{array}$

9. $4 \times 6 \times 5 =$ _____

10. $5 \times 2 \times 9 =$ _____

11. $400 \times 80 =$ _____

12. $\begin{array}{r} 206 \\ \times\ \ \ 5 \\ \hline \end{array}$

13. $\begin{array}{r} 298 \\ \times\ \ \ 9 \\ \hline \end{array}$

14. $\begin{array}{r} 859 \\ \times\ \ \ 6 \\ \hline \end{array}$

15. $\begin{array}{r} 67 \\ \times 42 \\ \hline \end{array}$

16. $\begin{array}{r} 53 \\ \times 59 \\ \hline \end{array}$

17. $\begin{array}{r} 364 \\ \times\ \ 43 \\ \hline \end{array}$

18. $\begin{array}{r} 3,856 \\ \times\ \ \ \ \ 56 \\ \hline \end{array}$

19. $\begin{array}{r} 725 \\ \times 684 \\ \hline \end{array}$

20. $\begin{array}{r} 3,849 \\ \times\ \ \ \ 545 \\ \hline \end{array}$

Divide. Show any remainders.

21. $4\overline{)25}$
22. $6\overline{)98}$
23. $7\overline{)704}$

24. $29\overline{)75}$
25. $49\overline{)877}$
26. $17\overline{)484}$

27. $75\overline{)2,760}$
28. $26\overline{)9,360}$
29. $32\overline{)39,490}$

Estimate the answer. Find the exact answer.

30.
$$\begin{array}{r} 876 \\ \times\ 58 \\ \hline \end{array}$$
Estimate
_____

31.
$$\begin{array}{r} 571 \\ \times\ 331 \\ \hline \end{array}$$
Estimate
_____

32.
$$\begin{array}{r} 6,284 \\ \times\ 683 \\ \hline \end{array}$$
Estimate
_____

33. $402\overline{)9,326}$
34. $579\overline{)79,420}$
35. $223\overline{)36,669}$

Between _____ and _____   Between _____ and _____   Between _____ and _____

Solve the following problems. Write your multiplication or division equation.

36. Mr. Martin has a barbershop. He can give 3 haircuts an hour. How many haircuts can he give in 7 hours?

    _____

37. Ed drove 330 miles. He used 15 gallons of gas. How many miles did he get to the gallon?

    _____

38. Ms. Parker can type 5 pages an hour. How many pages can she type in 42 hours?

    _____

39. Andrew drove 295 miles in 5 hours. What was his average speed?

    _____

40. Turkey cost $3 a pound on sale. Nancy bought 8 pounds of turkey. How much did she spend?

    _____

41. Laura's car payment is $235 a month. How much does she pay each year?

    _____

42. Duane worked 33 days. He made $1584. How much money did he make each day?

    _____

Word list

Add To put numbers together. To find the sum or total. The sign for adding is +.

Digit Any number from 0 through 9.

Division A short way to subtract. We divide to find how many groups of one number there are in a larger number. The signs for division are ÷ and $\overline{)}$.

Estimate To find an answer by rounding one or more of the numbers in a problem. We estimate when we do not need an exact answer.

Greater than The meaning of the sign >.

Hundreds The place value of the second digit to the left of the ones.

Key words The numbers and words in a problem which are needed to solve the problem.

Less than The meaning of the sign <.

Multiplication A short way to add. The sign for multiplication is ×. $6 + 6 + 6 + 6 = 6 \times 4$.

Multiplier The number by which we are multiplying.

Number line A line with numbers evenly spaced along it. A number line can be used to add, subtract, multiply, or divide.

Number sentence A sentence with numbers instead of words. Each number sentence must use =, <, or > to show how the numbers are related.

Ones The place value of a one-digit number.

Place value The worth given to a digit depending on its place in a number.

Remainder The number left over in a division problem.

Rename To write a number a different way, showing more ones, tens, hundreds, and so on.

Round To express a number to the nearest ten, hundred, thousand, and so on.

Subtract To take away one number from another. To find the difference between two numbers. To find how much more or less one number is than another. The sign for subtracting is −.

Sum The answer to an addition problem.

Tens The place value of the first digit to the left of the ones.

Thousands The place value of the third digit to the left of the ones.

Pretest/Unit 1/pages 1-2

1. 23
2. 68
3. 92
4. forty-seven
5. eighty-one
6. fifty-six
7. 4, 6, 7, 9
8. 9, 0, 6, 7
9. 4, 8, 9, 0
10. 50,498
11. 800,007,407
12. One thousand, four hundred ninety-two
13. Nine thousand, seventy
14. >
15. >
16. >
17. 567, 576, 657, 765
18. 5,089; 5,090; 5,900; 5,908
19. 3
20. 3
21. 2
22. 5
23. 8
24. 0
25. 5
26. 4
27. 8
28. 556,000; 555,800
29. 36,000,000; 35,910,000
30. A's Electronics
31. 58, 85, 102, 179, 197, 221, 362, 463, 464, 591
32. 93, 91, 87, 79, 67

Lesson 1/pages 3-5

1. 10
2. 60
3. 20
4. 70
5. 30
6. 80
7. 40
8. 90
9. 50
10. 100
11. 23
12. 67
13. 56
14. 91
15. 8 tens, 7 ones
16. 6 tens, 0 ones
17. 4 tens, 9 ones
18. 7 tens, 8 ones
19. 48

20. 39
21. 93
22. 26
23. 62
24. 50
25. 77
26. 83
27. twenty-nine
28. forty-two
29. ninety-nine
30. seventy-six
31. sixty-five
32. fifty-three
33. thirty
34. eighty-six
35. 62; 68
36. 82; 42; 92; 12
37. 89; 79
38. 45; 49
39. 89; 82; 88
40. 63; 23; 93
41. 76; 56; 16
42. 90; 94; 93
43. 17 14 12
44. 75 25
45. 20 + 2
46. 20 + 6
47. 60 + 2
48. 60 + 6
49. 70 + 1
50. 90 + 8
51. 80 + 2
52. 10 + 6
53. 30 + 3
54. 70 + 7
55. 40 + 3
56. 50 + 1
57. 30 + 4
58. 90 + 4
59. 10 + 3

Life Skill/pages 6-7

1. No
2. 817 W. Peach & 819 W. Peach
3. No
4. No
5. No
6. 16 N. Church & 18 N. Church
7. 509 E. Maple & 514 E. Maple
8. No
9. 2020 Ave. A & 2224 Ave. A
10. No
11. 516 S. Penn & 918 S. Penn
12. No
13. 730 Worth St. & 648 Worth St.
14. No

15. 23 Court Ave. & 145 Court Ave.
16. 1425 Knight & 207 Knight
17. 2 blocks
18. 7 blocks
19. 5 blocks
20. 7 blocks
21. No
22. Across the street
23. b
24. 7 blocks

Lesson 2/pages 8-9

1. 3, 0, 7
2. 7, 3, 9
3. 4, 5, 0
4. 6, 9, 8
5. 3, 4, 5, 6
6. 5, 0, 7, 3
7. 4, 3, 8, 9
8. 7, 9, 0, 2
9. 809; 899
10. 4,873; 4,442
11. 4,290; 2,285; 267
12. 1,100; 1,010
13. one thousand, three hundred forty-nine
14. three thousand, five hundred four
15. six thousand, forty-two
16. seven thousand, three hundred ninety
17. 2,485
18. 7,003
19. 3,207
20. 6,100

Lesson 3/pages 10-12

1. >
2. <
3. >
4. <
5. <
6. <
7. <
8. >
9. <
10. <
11. <
12. <
13. <
14. >
15. >
16. 3
17. 35
18. 90
19. 365

20. 7
21. 98
22. 100
23. 5,744
24. $11
25. $23
26. $11
27. $40
28. left
29. right
30. right
31. left
32. right
33. left
34. right
35. right
36. 468, 469, 470, 471, 472, 473
37. CP62741, CP62742, CP62743, CP62744, CP62745, CP62746
38. Suit B
39. 73
40. 50 inches, 55 inches, 58 inches, 60 inches
41. Matt

Life Skill/page 13

1. 11/28/65 [1 1] [2 8] [6 5]
2. 4/1/97 [0 4] [0 1] [9 7]
3. 12/31/84 [1 2] [3 1] [8 4]
4. 3/4/94 [0 3] [0 4] [9 4]
5. December 28, 1947
6. April 19, 1995
7. August 5, 1982
8. December 9, 1988

Lesson 4/pages 14-15

	Millions	Thousands	Ones
1.	74	957	89
2.	978	675	9
3.	392	7	856

4. 4
5. 3
6. 9
7. 3
8. 4
9. 9
10. 3
11. 6
12. 9
13. 5
14. 8
15. 0
16. 0
17. 4
18. 3
19. 9
20. 1
21. 7
22. 387,890,642; 980,732,500
23. 939,763,984
24. 35,482,409; 5,678,923
25. 4,798,042; 7,794,053
26. 1,000,000
27. 10,000
28. 100,000,000
29. 111,000,011

Life Skill/pages 16-17

1. 59621
2. 59943; 322
3. 60257; 314
4. 60780; 523
5. 61708; 928

Lesson 5/pages 18-20

1. $60
2. $680
3. $1,400
4. $14,910
5. $400
6. $900
7. $5,600
8. 45,000; 44,900
9. 99,000; 98,600
10. 105,000; 105,100
11. 45,000,000; 44,660,000
12. 305,000,000; 304,570,000
13. 60,000,000; 60,100,000
14. $800
15. $7,000
16. 30,000 feet
17. 600,000 square miles
18. 2,600 miles

Lesson 6/pages 21-22

1. $40
2. 56 hours
3. Electronics Plus
4. 3 hundreds; 9 ones
5. Tommy, Shane, Jessie, Margie, Bill
6. rent, electric, phone
7. Patrick
8. 9
9. $75,000
10. $80

Posttest/Unit 1/pages 23-24

1. 12
2. 9
3. 0
4. 19
5. 59
6. 325
7. 560,049
8. 900,013,006
9. seven
10. three
11. eighteen
12. ten
13. ninety-two
14. four hundred five
15. eight thousand, seven hundred sixty-four
16. one million, three hundred forty thousand
17. 27; 77
18. 65
19. 44
20. 9,975; 8,904; 6,908
21. 8,769; 8,606
22. 4
23. 0
24. 4
25. 5
26. 2
27. 2
28. 9
29. 8; 7
30. 14; 23
31. 351; 360
32. 99
33. 23; 999
34. 1,001
35. 1,020; 1,021; 1,121
36. 999; 9,099; 9,909
37. 665,566,000; 665,600,000; 670,000,000
38. 38,000,000; 37,570,000; 37,567,600
39. 60″, 65″, 69″, 72″, 75″
40. Ed

Pretest/Unit 2/pages 25-26

1. 3
2. 8
3. six
4. eleven
5. 10
6. 14
7. 15
8. 6
9. 12
10. 16
11. 13
12. 11
13. 6
14. 14
15. 500
16. 86
17. 763
18. 3
19. 9
20. 8
21. 7
22. 48

25. 97
26. 782
27. 7,382
28. 19,548
29. 2,041
30. 3,994
31. $32
32. $1,824
33. 4,519 bags
34. 156,000; 155,449
35. 465,000; 464,344
36. $1,050,000

Lesson 18/pages 59-60

1. 118
2. 127
3. 137
4. 158
5. 143
6. 980
7. 617
8. 744
9. 92 points
10. $167
11. $36
12. 74 miles
13. $230

Lesson 19/pages 61-63

1. 1,025
2. 1,514
3. 1,202
4. 1,347
5. 1,126
6. 1,430
7. 1,294
8. 1,483
9. 4,322
10. 5,841
11. 7,293
12. 9,462
13. 9,612
14. 4,460
15. 8,730
16. 4,512
17. $550
18. $544
19. $244
20. $1346
21. $4860
22. $15,020
23. $7,240
24. $21,423
25. 3,861 people
26. 1,230 miles
27. $2,141

Lesson 20/pages 64-65

1. 20
2. 30
3. 21
4. 26
5. 126
6. 199
7. 243
8. 242
9. 1,248
10. 3,460
11. 4,163
12. 4,896
13. 1,512
14. 1,441
15. 748
16. 1,842
17. 2,407
18. 5,732
19. 6,362
20. 8,610
21. 3,588
22. 5,669
23. 7,517
24. 4,436
25. 1,686
26. 694
27. 2,134
28. 2,431

Life Skill/page 66

1. 22 miles
2. 23 miles
3. 12 miles
4. 39 miles

5. 27 miles
6. Answers will vary.

Lesson 21/pages 67-68

1. 103,580
2. 523,584
3. 1,871,895
4. 19,552
5. 570,630
6. 891,331
7. 926,200
8. 1,283,751
9. 15,129,110
10. 1,799,263
11. 3,680,810
12. 62,237
13. 4,053,437
14. $115,530
15. $24,643
16. $32,335
17. 1,013,883 records

Life Skill/page 69

1. $628
2. $647
3. $609
4. $778
5. $2,662
6. $996
7. $377
8. $125
9. $183
10. $139
11. $234
12. $75
13. $370
14. $1,503
15. $2,499

Lesson 22/pages 70-71

1. $210; 204
2. 500; 499
3. 2,300; 2,302
4. $3,900; 3,895
5. $57,000; 57,464

Life Skill/page 72

Saturday
Breakfast: 470
Lunch: 483
Dinner: 509
Total: 1,462

Sunday
Breakfast: 245
Lunch: 423
Dinner: 456
Total: 1,124

Weekend total: 2,586

Posttest/Unit 3/pages 73-74

1. 14
2. 16
3. 10
4. 5
5. 79
6. 88
7. 689
8. 969

9. 97
10. 71
11. 132
12. 126
13. 673
14. 833
15. 1,252
16. 1,470
17. 4,765
18. 7,545
19. 16,423
20. 14,312
21. 566
22. 1,999
23. 6,296
24. 8,993
25. 19,552
26. 570,630
27. 3,680,810
28. 62,237
29. 4,053,437
30. 58 people
31. $820
32. $72
33. $590
34. about 121,000
35. 102,339 people; about 103,000 people

Pretest/Unit 4/pages 75-76

1. 7
2. 2
3. 6
4. 7
5. 45
6. 23
7. 63
8. 30
9. 121
10. 316
11. 219
12. 441
13. 29
14. 26
15. 275
16. 153
17. 385
18. 179
19. 4,656
20. 5,287
21. 4,889
22. 4,051
23. 4,867
24. 4,931
25. 22,191
26. 28,675
27. 34,878
28. 36,643
29. 188,938
30. 484,692
31. $27
32. $554
33. 1605
34. $266
35. 19
36. 54,000
37. 20,000

Lesson 23/pages 77-78

1. 1 13
2. 8 15
3. 4 10
4. 3 14
5. 7 12
6. 6 11
7. 1 18
8. 2 17
9. 2 16
10. 4 17
11. 8 13
12. 7 18
13. 3 15
14. 5 10
15. 7 11
16. 8 12
17. 1 17
18. 4 14

19. 7 11 **23.** 6 16
20. 8 10 **24.** 3 12
21. 5 13 **25.** 6 14
22. 2 15

Lesson 24/pages 79-80

1. 29 **11.** 1,432
2. 45 **12.** 6,834
3. 58 **13.** $382
4. 89 **14.** $85
5. 55 **15.** $67
6. 18 **16.** $129
7. 57 **17.** $35
8. 27 **18.** $329
9. 212 **19.** $1,745
10. 246 **20.** $1,803

Life Skill/page 81

1. $1.44 **4.** $2.90
2. $1.15 **5.** $.42
3. $.29 **6.** $3.15

Lesson 25/pages 82-83

1. 368 **12.** 683
2. 478 **13.** 5,734
3. 267 **14.** 5,677
4. 275 **15.** 3,469
5. 243 **16.** 1,929
6. 87 **17.** $441
7. 568 **18.** $57
8. 377 **19.** $245
9. 3,409 **20.** 1,299 sq. mi.
10. 3,343 **21.** 176 yrs.
11. 5,929 **22.** $4,079

Lesson 26/page 84

1. 689
2. 133
3. 2,323
4. 1,446
5. 8,447
6. 215
7. 5,215
8. 488 campsites
9. 33 years

Lesson 27/page 85

1. √ **7.** 6,366
2. 3,175 **8.** √
3. 303 **9.** √
4. √ **10.** √
5. 4,049 **11.** 222
6. √ **12.** √

Lesson 28/pages 86-87

1. 4,651,321 **4.** 50,114
2. 39,893,993 **5.** 913
3. 5,783,231 **6.** 88,679

7. 10,650 **13.** 306,111,089
8. 432,379 **14.** 551
9. 72,213,302 **15.** 1,520,610
10. 4,104,030 **16.** 4,487,360
11. 285,495 **17.** 2,790,263
12. 23,767,309 **18.** 4,703,435

Lesson 29/pages 88-90

1. 420; 419
2. 790; 790
3. 320; 317
4. 700; 639
5. 9,300; 9,276
6. 1,800; 1,810
7. 18,000; 17,735
8. 38,000; 37,762
9. 12,000; 12,513
10. $80
11. 360 vehicles
12. 1,200 stamps

Lesson 30/pages 91-92

1. $46
2. $49,000
3. $485
4. $5,300
5. $322

Posttest/Unit 4/pages 93-94

1. 7 **21.** 5,678
2. 5 **22.** 5,549
3. 6 **23.** 2,686
4. 9 **24.** 1,811
5. 43 **25.** 22,092
6. 32 **26.** 17,452
7. 25 **27.** 54,867
8. 10 **28.** 20,686
9. 231 **29.** 194,811
10. 611 **30.** 475,097
11. 319 **31.** 956,442
12. 111 **32.** 29,622,238
13. 36 **33.** $70
14. 26 **34.** $14
15. 329 **35.** $445
16. 55 **36.** $35
17. 552 **37.** 26 dozen
18. 69 **38.** 1,510 years
19. 5,488 **39.** $75,000
20. 4,479

Addition and Subtraction Posttest/pages 95-96

1. 45
2. 165
3. fifty-eight
4. eight thousand, six hundred fifty-two
5. >
6. <

7. 1 (tens) 5 (thousands)
8. 9 (tens) 4 (thousands)
9. 50,000,000; 49,800,000
10. 302,000,000; 302,160,000
11. 34
12. 110
13. 36
14. 50
15. 42
16. 768
17. 217
18. 901
19. 405
20. 334
21. 53
22. 118
23. 125
24. 986
25. 2,987
26. 94,931
27. 7,892
28. 1,184,636
29. 10,097
30. 38,300,795
31. 5 + 10 = 15
    10 + 5 = 15
    15 − 10 = 5
    15 − 5 = 10
32. 305,000 tickets
33. 46,779 children
34. 100,960 adults
35. 94,146 tickets

Pretest/Unit 5/pages 97-98

1. 5 **23.** 9
2. 54 **24.** 1
3. 40 **25.** 6 × 8 = 48
4. 12   8 × 6 = 48
5. 21   48 ÷ 6 = 8
6. 20   48 ÷ 8 = 6
7. 36 **26.** 12
8. 9 **27.** 9
9. 49 **28.** 7
10. 72 **29.** 7
11. 0 **30.** 6
12. 25 **31.** 1
13. 5 **32.** 3
14. 3 **33.** 40
15. 9 **34.** 5
16. 7 **35.** 9
17. 8 **36.** 1
18. 9 **37.** 3
19. 4 **38.** $63
20. 5 **39.** 9 pages
21. 0 **40.** $8
22. 6 **41.** $12

Lesson 31/pages 99-101

1. 6;6;3 **4.** 8;8;4
2. 10;10;5 **5.** 12;12;6
3. 14;14;7 **6.** 16;16;8

7. 9;9
8. 18;18
9. 27;27
10. 12;12
11. 21;21
12. 3;3
13. 15;15
14. 24;24
15. 0;0
16. 25
17. 14
18. 7
19. 30
20. 21
21. 48
22. 35
23. 28
24. 64
25. 40
26. 35
27. 72
28. 45
29. 42
30. 9
31. 0
32. 49
33. 18
34. 42
35. 56
36. 27
37. 48
38. 63
39. 36
40. 54
41. 0
42. 45
43. 32
44. 40
45. 54
46. $28
47. $20
48. $48
49. $15
50. 12 pounds

Lesson 32/pages 102-103

1. 3
2. 4
3. 5
4. 6
5. 7
6. 8
7. 2
8. 2
9. 2
10. 3
11. 3
12. 3
13. 4
14. 4
15. 4
16. 5
17. 5
18. 5
19. 6
20. 6
21. 6
22. 7
23. 7
24. 7
25. 8
26. 8
27. 8
28. 9
29. 9
30. 9
31. $36 ÷ 4 = $9
32. $24 ÷ 3 = $8
33. $18 ÷ $2 = 9 machines

Life Skill/pages 104-105

1. 16 tablets
2. 2 tablets
3. No
4. 4 pm
5. 6 hrs.
6. None
7. 8 dosages
8. 2 tsp.
9. 1 tsp.
10. No
11. No
12. 8 hrs.
13. No
14. 6 hrs.

Lesson 33/pages 106-107

1. 16;16;8;2
2. 12;12;3;4
3. 18;18;3;6
4. 9;3;27;27
5. 6;9;54;54
6. 8;8;6;6
7. 9;72;9;8
8. 2;2;7;7
9. 4;20;5;20
10. 2
11. 0
12. 0
13. 2
14. 36
15. 7
16. 4
17. 7
18. 6
19. 9
20. 4
21. 6
22. 5
23. 1
24. 9
25. 6
26. 15
27. 9
28. 27
29. 30
30. 8
31. $7 \times 8 = 56$
   $8 \times 7 = 56$
   $56 \div 7 = 8$
   $56 \div 8 = 7$
32. $4 \times 9 = 36$
   $9 \times 4 = 36$
   $36 \div 4 = 9$
   $36 \div 9 = 4$
33. $5 \times 8 = 40$
   $8 \times 5 = 40$
   $40 \div 8 = 5$
   $40 \div 5 = 8$
34. $6 \times 7 = 42$
   $7 \times 6 = 42$
   $42 \div 6 = 7$
   $42 \div 7 = 6$
35. $9 \times 3 = 27$
   $3 \times 9 = 27$
   $27 \div 3 = 9$
   $27 \div 9 = 3$
36. $5 \times 6 = 30$
   $6 \times 5 = 30$
   $30 \div 5 = 6$
   $30 \div 6 = 5$

Life Skill/page 108

1. 11
2. 18
3. 54
4. 24
5. 14
6. 320
7. 20
8. 19
9. 8
10. 192

Lesson 34/pages 109-110

1. $1 \times 2; 2 \times 1$
2. 8;3;8
3. 8
4. 12
5. 16
6. 20
7. 24
8. 28
9. 1
10. 2
11. 3
12. 30
13. 5
14. 6
15. 7
16. 7
17. 8
18. 9
19. 8
20. 6
21. ÷
22. ×
23. ×
24. ÷
25. ÷
26. ÷

27. ×
28. ÷
29. ×
30. ×
31. ×
32. ×
33. ÷
34. ÷
35. ×
36. $18 \div 3 = 6$
   $18 \div 6 = 3$
37. $72 \div 9 = 8$
   $72 \div 8 = 9$
38. $35 \div 7 = 5$
   $35 \div 5 = 7$
39. $12 \div 4 = 3$
   $12 \div 3 = 4$

Lesson 35/pages 111-113

1. 886
2. 44,958
3. 2,069
4. 9,216
5. 906
6. 961
7. 58,744 people
8. 488 cards
9. 770 pages
10. 160 miles

Lesson 36/pages 114-115

1. 65
2. 3,696
3. 430,621
4. 654
5. 665,667
6. 564
7. 191 CDs
8. 129 pounds
9. 21 tables
10. 22 flowers

Lesson 37/pages 116-117

1. 21 haircuts
2. 20 pages
3. $4 each
4. $1.09
5. 81 credits
6. 800
7. 900

Posttest/Unit 5/page 118

1. 6
2. 24
3. 21
4. 45
5. 30
6. 64
7. 81
8. 56
9. 8
10. 2
11. 9
12. 7
13. 9
14. 8
15. 5
16. 9
17. $7 \times 9 = 63$
   $9 \times 7 = 63$
   $63 \div 9 = 7$
   $63 \div 7 = 9$
18. 6
19. 4
20. 7
21. 9
22. 1
23. 7
24. 6
25. 40
26. 4
27. 8
28. 3
29. 5
30. c
31. a

Pretest/Unit 6/page 119-120

1.	72	11.	64
2.	245	12.	72
3.	783	13.	280
4.	618	14.	108
5.	2,390	15.	250
6.	5,478	16.	14,000
7.	2,760	17.	300,000
8.	1,519	18.	180
9.	72	19.	4,500
10.	315	20.	400,000

	Estimate	Exact
21.	2,400	2,400
22.	240,000	238,032
23.	50,000	58,851
24.	900,000	900,812
25.	4,056	
26.	1,175	
27.	3,654	
28.	40,204	
29.	44,116	
30.	77,418	
31.	230,577	
32.	5,461,692	
33.	1,835,570	
34.	$324	
35.	$2,820	
36.	$81,765	

Lesson 38/pages 121-122

1.	132	10.	388
2.	287	11.	1,284
3.	260	12.	672
4.	294	13.	690
5.	456	14.	736
6.	612	15.	$230
7.	511	16.	$828
8.	276	17.	$1.72
9.	190	18.	$6,860

Lesson 39/page 123

1.	48	5.	252
2.	126	6.	42
3.	192	10.	$224
4.	120	11.	60¢

Life Skill/pages 124-125

1.	$65	5.	$245
2.	$156	6.	$126
3.	$91	7.	Yes
4.	Family		

Lesson 40/pages 126-127

1.	200	7.	560
2.	60	8.	180
3.	240	9.	60
4.	250	10.	300
5.	210	11.	320
6.	360	12.	210

13.	800	22.	14,000
14.	2,400	23.	240,000
15.	3,000	24.	1,000,000
16.	3,600	25.	$2,000
17.	4,200	26.	$12,000
18.	3,600	27.	$150
19.	8,000	28.	$20,000
20.	60,000	29.	$50,000
21.	48,000		

Life Skill/page 128

1.	$56	7.	$336
2.	$48	8.	$1,344
3.	$64	9.	$96
4.	$64	10.	$360
5.	$56		$1,440
6.	$48		

Lesson 41/pages 129-130

1.	1,632	10.	125,064
2.	3,612	11.	96,662
3.	2,263	12.	314,340
4.	12,768	13.	$540
5.	6,045	14.	$780
6.	22,260	15.	$12,272
7.	19,536	16.	$7,250
8.	17,228	17.	$27,986
9.	26,174		

Life Skill/page 131

1.	$900	15.	$440
2.	$250	16.	$145
3.	$95	17.	$298
4.	$43	18.	$275
5.	$21	19.	$115
6.	$15	20.	$18
7.	$1,324	21.	$3,524
8.	$675	22.	$1,125
9.	$105	23.	$35
10.	$780	24.	$520
11.	$2,104	25.	$1,680
12.	$1,275	26.	$5,204
13.	$200	27.	$1,245
14.	$758	28.	$2,233

Lesson 42/page 132

1.	57,912	4.	139,004
2.	127,232	5.	507,872
3.	153,216	6.	199,867

Lesson 43/page 133

1.	116,076	4.	4,509,472
2.	476,634	5.	2,770,632
3.	60,495	6.	7,872,630

Lesson 44/pages 134-135

	Estimate	Exact
1.	3,000	3,087
2.	2,800	2,516

3.	20,000	21,801
4.	56,000	53,406
5.	15,000	14,725
6.	200,000	170,976
7.	450,000	436,632
8.	90,000	130,524
9.	360,000	371,811
10.	1,800,000	1,762,992
11.	4,000,000	4,474,230
12.	1,000,000	1,151,772
13.	$250	$240
14.	$7,500	$7,540

Lesson 45/pages 136-137

1.	$23
2.	$710
3.	$350
4.	$34,500
5.	$36

Posttest/Unit 6/pages 138-139

1.	138	11.	225
2.	490	12.	160
3.	783	13.	162
4.	1,001	14.	56
5.	2,790	15.	200
6.	4,963	16.	540
7.	6,744	17.	3,000
8.	9,710	18.	6,000
9.	120	19.	280,000
10.	84	20.	800,000

	Estimate	Exact
21.	700	938
22.	27,000	23,244
23.	200,000	173,136
24.	60,000	72,292
25.	180,000	185,592
26.	2,000,000	1,980,807
27.	552	
28.	37,536	
29.	184,002	
30.	68,303	
31.	4,059,678	
32.	1,703,502	
33.	3,629,679	
34.	1,846,386	
35.	3,540,240	
36.	$52	
37.	$200	
38.	$240,690	
39.	7,250	
40.	27,986	

Pretest/Unit 7/pages 140-141

1.	8 R1	7.	169 R3
2.	8 R3	8.	44 R7
3.	11 R2	9.	14 R7
4.	3 R2	10.	115 R83
5.	3 R5	11.	125 R9
6.	81 R5	12.	124 R9

13. 694 R25
14. 64 R2
15. 41 R3
16. 135 R9
17. 216 R6
18. 53 R437
19. Between 200 and 300
20. Between 200 and 300
21. Between 5 and 6
22. Between 20 and 30
23. 85 R1
24. 792 R52
25. 20
26. $850
27. 67 sets
28. $45
29. 42 tickets

Lesson 46/pages 142-144

1. $9\overline{)81}$ (quotient 9)
2. $3\overline{)24}$ (quotient 8)
3. $4\overline{)12}$ (quotient 3)
4. 48 ÷ 6 = 8
5. 56 ÷ 7 = 8
6. 40 ÷ 5 = 8
7. $9\overline{)36}$ (quotient 4)
8. 72 ÷ 8 = 9
9. 45 ÷ 9 = 5
10. $7\overline{)42}$ (quotient 6)
11. $6\overline{)42}$ (quotient 7)
12. 54 ÷ 6 = 9
13. 9
14. 8
15. 9
16. 4 R2
17. 7 R2
18. 6 R4
19. 6 R3
20. 5 R1
21. 3
22. 7 R3
23. 4 R2
24. 5 R8
25. 9 games
    2 people
26. 109 cars
27. 4 shelves
28. 22 bulbs
29. 7 poems
30. 152 miles/day

Lesson 47/pages 145-146

1. 23 R1
2. 11
3. 26
4. 23

5. 14
6. 10 R8
7. 12 R5
8. 26 R1
9. 11 R7
10. 17 sacks; 2 pounds
11. 16 pictures
12. 8 bags, 31 cans

Lesson 48/pages 147-148

1. 49
2. 61
3. 99
4. 47
5. 81 R4
6. 23 R3
7. 81 R1
8. 82 R1
9. 234
10. 239
11. 131
12. 193
13. 277 R1
14. 124 R4
15. 101
16. 123 R1
17. 69 bills
18. 142 sets
    1 shirt left
19. 18 miles/gallon

Lesson 49/Pages 149-151

1. 198 R1
2. correct
3. 321 R1
4. correct
5. 1,157
6. 116 R8
7. 1,853 R3
8. 1,059 R1
9. 812 R1
10. 1,432
11. correct
12. 146 R6
13. correct
14. 1,421
15. correct
16. 3,819
17. $431
18. 211 weeks
19. 233 boxes

Life Skill/page 152

1. $270
2. $100
3. $370
4. $2,700
5. 5 terms
6. $1,100

Lesson 50/pages 153-154

1. 3
2. 6
3. 4
4. 3
5. 5 R12
6. 3 R5
7. 2 R24
8. 3 R15
9. 2 R21
10. 3 R14
11. 2 R31
12. 5 R11
13. 7 R10
14. 6 R6
15. 2 R5
16. 6
17. 3 R21
18. 3 R4
19. 6 R2
20. 3 R15

21. $3
22. 3 pieces each
    3 left over
23. 8 miles/gallon
24. 6 bags
    7 pounds left over

Life Skill/page 155

1. $500
2. 30 weeks
3. $31.50
4. $125/month
5. $420

Lesson 51/pages 156-158

1. Between 10 and 20
   19 R11
2. Between 20 and 30
   24 R18
3. Between 20 and 30
   21 R40
4. Between 10 and 20
   12 R7
5. Between 10 and 20
   11 R52
6. Between 10 and 20
   12 R38
7. Between 10 and 20
   12 R63
8. Between 10 and 20
   11 R48
9. Between 20 and 30
   21 R6
10. Between 10 and 20
    11 R3
11. Between 100 and 200
    133 R4
12. Between 100 and 200
    126 R5
13. Between 1 and 100
    82 R36
14. Between 1 and 100
    71 R43
15. 31 boxes
    6 cards remaining
16. 252 boxes

Lesson 52/pages 159-160

1. 8
2. 5
3. 9
4. 6 R14
5. 7 R14
6. 8 R23
7. 27
8. 24
9. 61 R461
10. $25
11. 5 days

Life Skill/page 161

1. $931
2. $65
3. $63

4. $490
5. $384
6. Answers may vary.

Lesson 53/pages 162-163

1. 504
2. 309
3. 705
4. 40
5. 80 R7
6. 70 R6
7. 50 R11
8. 80 R8
9. 30 R7
10. 708 R2
11. 606 R2
12. 701 R2
13. 302
14. 106 R3
15. 409 R10

Life Skill/page 164

1. $426
2. $142
3. $158
4. $52.67
5. $138
6. $46
7. $162
8. $54
9. $474
10. $158
11. $60
12. $20
13. $159
14. $53
15. $222
16. $74

Lesson 54/pages 165-166

1. $119,451
2. $8,258
3. $416,148
4. $235,859
5. $45
6. $240
7. 77 children
8. 38 shirts
9. 16 miles/gallon

Posttest/Unit 7/pages 167-168

1. 7
2. 323 R6
3. 194 R2
4. 9 R2
5. 132 R2
6. 541 R7
7. 3 R14
8. 233 R29
9. 488 R11
10. 3 R9
11. 431 R11
12. 218 R10
13. 114 R2
14. 53 R101
15. 103
16. 26
17. 331
18. 341 R382
19. Between 10 and 20
20. Between 50 and 60
21. Between 100 and 200
22. Between 200 and 300
23. 2 R20

24. 16 R3
25. 20 R1
26. 31
27. 101 R1
28. 236
29. 16 miles/gallon
30. $43
31. 409 miles/day
32. $50
33. $8,350

Pretest/Unit 8/pages 169-170

1. 4^3
2. 5^6
3. 8^2
4. 2^4
5. 25
6. 27
7. 10,000
8. 81
9. 10
10. 8
11. 26
12. 15
13. 90
14. 17
15. $x = 6$
16. $x = 27$
17. $y = 21$
18. $a = 6$
19. $n = 12$
20. $x = 25$
21. $z = 0$
22. $t = 10$
23. $v = 4$
24. $r = 25$
25. $m = 18$
26. $j = 9$
27. $p = 19$
28. $r = 39$
29. $b = 8$
30. $n = 50$
31. $250 - 209 = x$; $41
32. $399 - 30 = x$; $369

Lesson 55/pages 171-172

1. 5^2
2. 7^4
3. 3^3
4. 10^2
5. 1^6
6. 6^6
7. 2^5
8. 0^4
9. 4^3
10. 8^5
11. 32
12. 16
13. 27
14. 49
15. 625
16. 64
17. 1
18. 1,000
19. 8
20. 16

Lesson 56/pages 173-174

1. Exponent
2. Parentheses (4 + 7)
3. Parentheses (10 − 8)
4. Multiplication 2 × 4
5. Addition 6 + 5
6. 23
7. 13
8. 30
9. 4
10. 11
11. 10
12. 14
13. 34
14. 12
15. 25
16. 12
17. 17
18. 17
19. 20
20. 3
21. 19
22. 11
23. 10
24. 14
25. 26

Lesson 57/page 175

1. 10
2. 15
3. 26
4. 30
5. 10
6. 7
7. 18
8. 28

Lesson 58/page 176

1. $x = 14$
2. $x = 10$
3. $x = 4$
4. $x = 23$
5. $x = 20$
6. $x = 11$
7. $x = 8$
8. $x = 21$
9. $x = 5$
10. $x = 16$
11. $x = 13$
12. $x = 23$
13. $x = 10$
14. $x = 25$
15. $x = 30$
16. $x = 26$

Lesson 59/page 177

1. 23
2. 8
3. 22
4. 21
5. 10
6. 35
7. 32
8. 12
9. 29
10. 31
11. 28
12. 22
13. 24
14. 24
15. 90
16. 48
17. 75
18. 45

Lesson 60/page 178

1. $x = 5$
2. $x = 3$
3. $a = 1$
4. $y = 7$
5. $p = 8$
6. $x = 6$

7. $a = 8$
8. $x = 5$
9. $x = 8$
10. $d = 5$
11. $f = 3$
12. $x = 1$
13. $x = 6$
14. $x = 8$

Lesson 61/page 179

1. $b = 24$ 8. $n = 60$
2. $x = 25$ 9. $a = 48$
3. $a = 12$ 10. $x = 100$
4. $d = 36$ 11. $y = 49$
5. $f = 45$ 12. $a = 90$
6. $n = 63$ 13. $x = 32$
7. $m = 121$ 14. $y = 32$

Lesson 62/pages 180-181

1. $8 - 5 = x$
   $x = \$3$
2. $80 - 12 = x$
   $x = \$68$
3. $1{,}550 - 1{,}200 = x$
   $x = \$350$
4. $12{,}995 - 1{,}500 = x$
   $x = \$11{,}495$
5. $650 + 125 = x$
   $x = \$775$
6. $30{,}000 - 24{,}600 = x$
   $x = \$5{,}400$

Posttest/Unit 8/pages 182-183

1. 5^2
2. 2^3
3. 9^3
4. 7^5
5. 36
6. 8
7. 81
8. 64
9. 19
10. 13
11. 33
12. 30
13. 80
14. 46
15. $x = 14$
16. $x = 38$
17. $y = 11$
18. $a = 4$
19. $p = 15$
20. $x = 28$
21. $z = 20$
22. $t = 32$
23. $v = 6$
24. $r = 22$
25. $m = 42$
26. $j = 8$
27. $p = 28$

28. $r = 39$
29. $b = 9$
30. $n = 162$
31. $450 - 399 = x$
    $x = \$51$
32. $110{,}000 - 5{,}000 = x$
    $x = \$105{,}000$

**Multiplication and Division
Posttest/pages 184-186**

1. 30
2. 405
3. 6
4. 3
5. $7 \times 9 = 63$
   $9 \times 7 = 63$
   $63 \div 7 = 9$
   $63 \div 9 = 7$
6. 399
7. 228
8. 168
9. 120
10. 90
11. 32,000
12. 1,030
13. 2,682
14. 5,154
15. 2,814
16. 3,127
17. 15,652
18. 215,936
19. 495,900
20. 2,097,705
21. 6 R1
22. 16 R2
23. 100 R4
24. 2 R17
25. 17 R44
26. 28 R8
27. 36 R60
28. 360
29. 1,234 R2

	Estimate	Exact
30.	54,000	50,808
31.	180,000	189,001
32.	4,200,000	4,291,972

33. Between 20 and 30
    23 R80
34. Between 100 and 200
    137 R97
35. Between 100 and 200
    164 R97
36. 21 haircuts
37. 22 miles/gallon
38. 210 pages
39. 59 miles/hour
40. $24
41. $2,820
42. $48